PITTSBURGH STEELERS GLORY DAYS

PITTSBURGH STEELERS GLORY DAYS

DALE GRDNIC

SPORTS PUBLISHING

Sports Publishing books may be purchased in bulk at special discounts for sales promotion, corporate gifts, fund-raising, or educational purposes. Special editions can also be created to specifications. For details, contact the Special Sales Department, Sports Publishing, 307 West 36th Street, 11th Floor, New York, NY 10018 or sportspubbooks@skyhorsepublishing.com.

Sports Publishing® is a registered trademark of Skyhorse Publishing, Inc.®, a Delaware corporation.

Visit our website at www.sportspubbooks.com

10 9 8 7 6 5 4 3 2 1

Library of Congress Cataloging-in-Publication Data is available on file.

ISBN: 978-1-61321-329-2

Printed in the United States of America

This book is dedicated to my wonderful wife, Denise, who has been my inspiration and sounding board for many stories over the years. I've known Denise for some nine years now, and she's always been my biggest fan. She says she loves me as much as the Steelers, but that probably depends on how well they're playing. It was tough for me during the 2005 Super Bowl run.

CONTENTS

FOREWORD

BY ANDY RUSSELL

UPON FIRST HEARING about Dale Grdnic's new book, *Pittsburgh Steelers Glory Days*, I thought, "Oh no, not another Steelers book!" I just wondered how many books our loyal fans could support as former players, retired announcers, and ex-newspaper writers have littered bookshelves trying to connect with the team's popularity.

Yet, I was wrong. What makes Dale's book most remarkable is that he has bravely attempted to involve the Steelers fans. Through their individual opinions—their feelings at a given moment, the personal or familial challenges they were facing, their location during that special game—Dale has comprised a list of the 20 greatest Pittsburgh Steelers games. Our fans were so hugely important in so many of those great games; and it is high time we reflect on their roles in all those victories.

For example, I will never forget how, in our turnaround year, 1972, when we were playing our nemesis, the Cleveland Browns (we had a few games left, but this was a crucial one), in Three Rivers Stadium, hoping to eventually win our first division title. Our great fans, a sellout crowd, were the loudest they have ever been. I remember thinking, "If we don't start performing better, our fans are going to come out onto the field and beat these Browns for us." It was an unbelievable feeling that motivated us even more—and all the players knew that our fans cared deeply, that it was every bit as important to them that we win as it was to us.

Of course, I would argue that most of those crucial games were played back in the early 1970s, when the team was going from perennial loser (we were referred to as "SOS," Same Old Steelers) to team of the decade. The city had struggled in the '50s and '60s by losing key businesses and seeing its steel industry nearly going into bankruptcy; but in the early 1970s, the city began to recover. The quality of life rebounded in our fine city: the development of the Cultural District, new stadiums, trees planted along our city streets, a complete urban renewal.

This comeback coincided with the Steelers' journey from a very bad team to a great team, and I believe the team became a symbol for the city's resurgence. We always had a loyal fan base of about 30,000 back in the '60s, and they had put up with some woeful incompetence. However, in the '70s, new fans embraced the team and became hugely committed to helping us reach our goal—an NFL championship. As Dale notes in this book, interviewing some of those so-committed fans revealed that they all had slightly different perspectives; but Steelers games on Sunday became part of their family ritual, whether it was at home, on television, or tailgating at the stadium.

It was an amazing transformation, starting with our brilliant new coach, Chuck Noll, a great teacher, and then continued with some of the greatest drafts ever seen in the NFL. From Joe Greene to Terry Bradshaw and on to Jack Ham, then Franco Harris, Jack Lambert, Lynn Swann, John Stallworth, and Mike Webster—all Hall of Famers—the team was blessed with too many other very gifted players to mention here. Only five of us who came from the pre-Noll era, including myself, survived the journey to the team's first NFL championship appearance in Super Bowl IX, where we beat the Vikings.

Interestingly, in regard to this book, probably none of the aforementioned players would agree on which game was the most important or how to rank those games in comparison. So many hugely important games played during the Coach Cowher regime that younger fans might consider them the most important games because they were there, and they participated in the victory.

Personally, I absolutely think that the most important game the Steelers ever played was the first one. Art Rooney (The Chief), as legend has it, had won the team in a card game; and it was clear that it would not be an easy road to success. That first game, played so many years ago—as The Chief worried how he would meet his payroll and how many fans would pay for seats—was a monumentally important Steelers game, perhaps the most meaningful ever. If the Chief had not had the courage of true American entrepreneurship he never would have backed that first game, risking I'm sure what, in those days, was quite a bit of money.

Yet, the quintessential game of the Steelers history, in my humble opinion, was the 1974 AFC championship game we played against the Oakland Raiders. Why? It was against a great Raiders team, one that had beaten us soundly in the previous year's playoffs, and they had just beaten the reigning two-time Super Bowl champion Miami Dolphins. We played them in their house, and most experts were picking the Raiders. We came together that day, though, and played an outstanding game to get into our first Super Bowl. Until you win a game like that, you really don't know whether you can; so it becomes a huge victory, making us all true believers in our winning destiny. Those teams went on to win four Super Bowls in six seasons.

In reading this book, however, you will discover that all our fans, including Dale Grdnic, have very different opinions as to which games were the most important to The Steelers Nation. Debate amongst yourselves, Steelers fans, because the nostalgia I felt reading your stories reminded me how important those games were to an entire city.

So, here's one guy who is very happy that there is one more Steelers book out, especially one as special as this one.

Andy Russell

PREFACE

FOR 75 YEARS, the Pittsburgh Steelers have cemented their role as one of pro football's most storied franchises—one that has given birth to the strongest fan base in history: The Steelers Nation. All Steelers fans have stories, whether they were present during the black-and-gold glory days, or they met their favorite players, or maybe, they even fell in love.

My best friend, Joe, and I used to drive the 90 minutes to Saint Vincent College with his siblings and their friends. After countless games, we would wait forever just to catch a glimpse of our heroes. Yet, my most amazing Steelers story came many years later. The first time I walked into their locker room to conduct interviews, only a few months removed from college graduation in 1981, was mystical. I worked in radio back then, and I couldn't believe that Terry Bradshaw, Jack Ham, Jack Lambert, Franco Harris, "Mean" Joe Greene, Dwight White, L.C. Greenwood, Rocky Bleier, and Mike Wagner were a mere arm's length away.

Another moment nearly two decades later, however, would surpass that thrill.

On June 9, 1998—several years after I returned to the Pittsburgh area as a sportswriter—I was covering a Steelers mini-camp workout for *The Patriot-News* in Harrisburg. I saw this girl doing interviews and found out her name was Denise. She was a sports writer for the *Daily News* in McKeesport, Pennsylvania.

We didn't start dating immediately, although Denise said she would have, had I only asked. She eventually did ask me out, though; and after several years and many games and training camps later, Denise and I were married when very few people even knew we were dating. We celebrated our five-year anniversary February 1, 2007.

Denise and I still watch Steelers games together, although we don't cover them together anymore. She went back to school and became a registered nurse in 2006. It's a much more rewarding career for Denise, but she can still attend home games as a fan, and she shares Steelers season tickets with her siblings.

I'm sure you all have your own special Steelers story, and I hope those shared with you in this book will help you recall them fondly. Stories just like yours helped create this collection of great moments, and they help us remember how closely intertwined our lives are with the rest of The Steelers Nation.

1

THE WAIT IS OVER

AFC Central Division Title Game
Jack Murphy Stadium
San Diego, California
December 17, 1972

WHILE HER MOTHER, Hilda, had a crush on Bobby Layne, the Pittsburgh Steelers quarterback from 1958-62, Carrie Barnes always leaned more toward the defensive side of the line. She still does to this day. She even owned a No. 75 Joe Greene jersey. Born and raised in Canonsburg, Pennsylvania—the oldest of Hilda and Charles Moyar's four children—Carrie couldn't remember a time that the Steelers didn't play an integral part in her life.

"We never had two cents to rub together, but we didn't know we were poor," Carrie said. "Yet, we always had the Steelers. Even before television, we used to have Sunday dinner at one o'clock, and the radio in the kitchen would be tuned in to the Steelers games. So it was a really big deal for us to listen to the games. Once we could afford a television, it was one of the highlights of our lives to watch the games. Those were the days, as they say."

But not for the Steelers—nearly 40 years of futility had extended from the day beloved owner Art Rooney Sr. founded the team in 1933. Only eight winning seasons were notched prior to Chuck Noll's arrival as head coach, and he didn't finish better than .500 until 1972, his fourth season.

None of that mattered to the Moyars, though. Along with strong family values, Hilda and Charles instilled a love for the Steelers at an early age, one that only grew over the years.

A year or so out of high school, Carrie married George Ramsey, and the two would spend a good deal of their time watching football together. They went to high school games on Friday nights, college football games at Pitt on Saturdays, and to Steelers games, of course, on Sundays. The Steelers played at Forbes Field, a stadium they shared with Major League Baseball's Pirates, and Pitt Stadium, which they shared with the Panthers.

"We all just loved football, all my friends," Carrie said. "The Steelers were so bad back then that you could walk right up to the gate before kickoff and buy good tickets. So that's what we'd do."

The Steelers, though, got a lot easier to watch in 1972.

Chuck Noll had Joe Greene anchoring his defense, a strong-armed Terry Bradshaw guiding his offense. He added defensive stalwarts like Mike Wagner, Jack Ham, Dwight White, and L.C. Greenwood, and offensive players like Jim Clack, Gerry Mullins, and Ron Shanklin made an early impact. Rookie running back Franco Harris had been taken in the first round of the 1972 NFL Draft as well, and the team was quickly on the rise. The players knew during training camp that it was only a matter of time before they would realize that success on the football field. Little did they know that it would happen so immediately.

The Steelers knocked off the Oakland Raiders, 34-28, in the season-opener at Three Rivers Stadium. The Raiders had just played in the Super Bowl a few years earlier and pounded the Steelers in their first meeting in Oakland in 1970, so the win signaled a change in Pittsburgh. Though the Steelers then lost at Cincinnati, 15-10, on five field goals, they won at St. Louis, before losing again the next week at Dallas, 17-13, on a gadget play. The Cowboys were the defending Super Bowl champs; so, even at 2-2, the Steelers were primed to make a run.

"Chuck had brought in a lot of talented guys to that point and got rid of a lot of older veterans who just weren't doing the job,"

Steelers linebacker Andy Russell said. "He cut guys while they were eating lunch. He didn't care. He wanted to field a winning team; and to do that, he had to bring in talented players who were winners— so that's what he did."

Russell was among the older veterans who predated Noll. Also surviving that first player purge were running back Rocky Bleier, punter Bobby Walden, offensive guard Sam Davis, and center Ray Mansfield. Those players, along with the talent assembled through the draft, elevated the Steelers' play on the field after that slow start. The Steelers reeled off five straight wins, including home games against Houston, New England, Cincinnati, and Kansas City—the Super Bowl IV winner—as well as Buffalo on the road.

The team traveled to Cleveland the ensuing week with renewed enthusiasm. At 7-2, the Steelers were dogfighting the Browns for the AFC Central Division title. Cleveland got the upper hand that day with a 26-24 win, but the Steelers were not discouraged. They knew they would get another shot at the Browns two weeks later in Pittsburgh.

"We always knew we had a good team; but we were really starting to believe after that little winning streak in 1972," said Mike Wagner. "We beat a couple good teams and lost to a couple, but our confidence was high. We got over the hump with that, and we were convinced that we could play with anybody on any given day. We had a chance to win the division on the field, and that's all that we really wanted."

The Steelers pounded the Vikings the following week to set up the rematch with Cleveland at Three Rivers Stadium, and it was no contest. The Steelers scored early and often, winning 30-0. They had the upper hand on the Browns in the AFC Central Division title chase and just had to win tough road games at Houston and the regular-season finale in San Diego to clinch the club's first division title. The Oilers game was a struggle, but the Steelers pulled out a 9-3 win on three Roy Gerela field goals. Everyone in the Steelers organization knew the enormity of the upcoming Chargers contest, and Noll quickly got the situation under control. In order to best prepare the Steelers for what essentially was a championship game, the club took Noll and his staff, the Steelers players, the radio broadcast team, all their families, and a media contingent to the West Coast a week early to acclimate everyone to the time change and the heat.

"We just felt that was the best way to handle things," said Dan Rooney, the owner's son. "The weather really wasn't too nice in Pittsburgh, and we had some injured players. So, we just felt that it would be a good thing to get out there and get some good work for such an important game."

It was a daunting task, to be sure, but everyone connected with the Steelers appeared to be up for the challenge.

"It was a nice week out there," Steelers radio commentator Myron Cope said. "But it was a big game, so practices were serious. The team worked very hard to get ready for this game. They knew what was at stake."

Actually, it wasn't all hard work for the Steelers. During one practice session, Cope showed up with a special guest. The night before, while out on the town, Cope had a note sent to Frank Sinatra, asking "Old Blue Eyes" to visit the practice session the next day to see Franco Harris. When Sinatra showed up, Cope had him installed as an officer in Franco's Italian Army—the rookie running back's fan club. Cope wanted to introduce Harris to Sinatra that day, but the shy rookie wouldn't leave the practice field. Finally, Noll sent Harris over to the sideline for a brief visit with Cope and Sinatra, but quickly called him back to the huddle.

Harris wasn't the only Steelers player with a fan club. There was Frenchy's Foreign Legion for running back John "Frenchy" Fuqua, Gerela's Gorillas for place-kicker Roy Gerela, Bradshaw's Brigade for quarterback Terry Bradshaw, and Ham's Hussars—named after a Polish Cavalry unit—for outside linebacker Jack Ham. A large battalion of fans made the march to California to see if the Steelers could clinch their first division title.

"This is the most excited I've ever been for one game," said Carrie Barnes-favorite, Joe Greene.

Safety Ralph "Sticks" Anderson intercepted Chargers quarterback John Hadl on the third play of the game and returned it to the 11-

yard line. Franco Harris would score three plays later to give the Steelers an early lead. The Steelers defense would rise to the occasion several times thereafter, as Ham, Mike Wagner, and cornerback Mel Blount each picked off a Hadl pass later in the game. A chorus of boos rained upon the quarterback from the San Diego fans while the Steelers faithful in attendance—reportedly some 1,200—cheered wildly every time their club made a big play.

Bradshaw was tackled in the end zone for a safety late in the first quarter, cutting the Steelers' lead to 7-2, but the team's opportunistic defense set up the offense again in the second. Bradshaw guided the Steelers deep into San Diego territory, and Fuqua crashed in from the 2-yard line to improve the team's advantage to 14-2 at halftime.

The Steelers defense tightened its screws even further in the second half. Tailback Mike Garrett—a former Heisman Trophy winner from USC and the AFC's third-leading rusher coming into the game—was held to just five yards on 14 attempts. His running mate, Cid Edwards, who'd entered the game with more than 600 rushing yards, ran for just 52 on 13 attempts. To hold the Chargers to 56 total rushing yards on 30 carries was remarkable, but the Steelers D was also working on another shutout of sorts: They had a chance to record their seventh (out of 14 total) game without allowing an offensive touchdown.

"Our defense [had] to be the best in football," said Ray Mansfield. "I think right after training camp, we knew we had a good football team."

Offensive tackle Larry Brown recovered a third-quarter fumble to retain possession, squashing San Diego's chances for redemption. Gerela then would kick a 26-yard field goal that kicked off the Steelers' celebration after three quarters. Gerela also had two field goals blocked, or he would have beaten out New York Jets place-kicker Bobby Howfield for the AFC scoring title. The Steelers offense, which usually relied on strong ground play by rookie runner Harris and big plays from Bradshaw, was not as efficient, which kept the score closer than it should have been.

Fuqua had just 51 yards rushing on 17 carries, and Harris was held to 34 on 15; but Harris entered the game with more than 1,000 yards rushing and finished the season with 1,055 (5.6 yards per carry) and 10 touchdowns to capture Offensive Rookie of the Year honors. However, his poor game against the Chargers did cause him to finish 51 yards short of Green Bay's John Brockington, who had set the NFL record for rookie running backs the previous season. Bradshaw completed 12 of 23 passes for 152 yards, and he wanted to finish the game on a positive note. So, when Blount's interception in the fourth quarter gave the Steelers good field position once again, Bradshaw took advantage, getting the Steelers into the red zone and, after faking a handoff to Harris, dropped back to pass from the 17.

After a horrendous rookie season in which he threw just six touchdown passes and 24 interceptions, Bradshaw had rebounded in 1971 to complete better than 54 percent of his passes for 2,259 yards and 13 touchdowns with 22 interceptions. Those numbers dropped drastically in 1972 as Harris and the running game emerged, but certainly better days were ahead for the big quarterback; and he finished with a bang against the Chargers. Bradshaw capped that late fourth-quarter drive by finding speedy wideout Ron Shanklin across the middle for his 12th touchdown pass.

The 24-2 victory capped an amazing season for the Steelers and their fans. The franchise had captured its first AFC Central Division title, and the long wait was over. The Steelers completed a stellar 11-3 season after winning just 11 combined games total in the previous two seasons and only 30 over the previous eight.

Andy Russell knew that Noll, the team's architect, deserved much credit for the success this season—and that it was a long time coming for him. ("This is the most I've seen Chuck smile in four years," Russell would joke.) However, he was quick to praise the man who stuck with the Steelers during trying times in those first few years. Russell noted that Noll never appeared to be out of touch with his players, always aware of what happened with them on and off the field, and he was able to combine the right mix of discipline and praise to get the most from his men. He wasn't one for big, long speeches or patting his players on the back. The players were there to do a job, and Noll was the man to coach them and bring them together.

Andy Russell survived a new Steelers coaching regime and was an integral part of the club's first AFC Central Division title in 1972.

The line between coach and player never blurred with Noll and the Steelers, and L.C. Greenwood agreed that was among Noll's finest qualities. Greenwood explained that Noll knew exactly how to maximize a player's potential, which wasn't always easy. "We had a bunch of guys where Chuck stirred the pot to get the guys that he wanted here, and they were a group that had a winning attitude," Greenwood said. "We wanted to win football games, and we didn't talk about losing games. That was all in the past. So, the attitude was much better, and everybody was very disappointed when we lost a football game. It was more disappointing to the players than it was to the coaches, and the city actually got a winning attitude as well. We weren't 'SOS'—the 'Same Old Steelers'— anymore. Guys went out to try to improve themselves. There were more after-practice workouts, early workouts, and everybody was in the film room and weight room for extra work."

While all the Steelers' hard work paid off with a division title, there was much more to accomplish. There were the AFC playoffs, another first for the Steelers, against the hated Oakland Raiders and maybe even a Super Bowl appearance in the future. The Steelers wanted to celebrate their big win and first division title for Art Rooney Sr., known as "The Chief." On the long flight back home, Andy Russell made sure the Steelers paid tribute to him.

"I know I speak for every member of this team when I award this game ball to The Chief," Russell said. "I can say that we all respect this man, and we love to play for him and work for him. He's waited a long time for this, and this is just the first of many (championships) to come."

Rooney Sr., along with those around him, was clearly moved by Russell's words, and dry eyes were hard to find on the plane.

"This is the finest present I have ever received," Rooney Sr. said. "I want to take this opportunity to congratulate you and thank you. I would like to thank all of you, the members of the coaching staff, the press, and all the fans in Pittsburgh and the tri-state area."

The Steelers' long wait for a division championship had finally ended.

Since so many tickets were available, Carrie Barnes didn't consider buying season tickets until after she and George divorced. After moving to Harrisburg in 1975, she formally applied for Steelers season tickets. Thanks to the 1972 division title and a 1974 Super Bowl championship, though, attendance had risen to a point that a lengthy waiting list had to be created to handle season-ticket requests. Carrie, however, was far from deterred. Year after year, the team would contact her to inform her she was still on the list, but they never told her how close.

In 1990, that note from the Steelers finally changed, and the wait was over. Carrie was told that she would receive two season tickets for the upcoming year. The price had increased since she first applied 15 years earlier, but Carrie didn't care. She cherishes those season tickets and can't wait for the renewal notice to arrive in the mail.

"My husband, Lee, can't believe I spend so much of my money on the Steelers, but they're my guys," Carrie said. "He calls the games a 'fat-boy joust'; but he doesn't understand. He doesn't really like football, but I just love it. I live for the Steelers and their games."

That is why Carrie makes the 224-mile trek—from her front door to a Liberty Avenue garage in downtown Pittsburgh where she parks—for every Steelers home game during football season. It's a straight shot, she said, and an easy drive on the Pennsylvania Turnpike that she picks up in Carlisle. She gets off at the Monroeville Exit and can have her car parked in less than three and a half hours driving time, which might appear to be excessive for some, but not a dedicated Steelers fan like Carrie Barnes.

"I've only missed a couple games over the years; and they take care of the Turnpike, so weather usually isn't a problem," Carrie said. "I leave the house before 7 a.m. for a 1 p.m. start and around 9 a.m. for a 4 p.m. game. I get home by 9 p.m. after a 1 p.m. start and 1 a.m. for a 4 p.m. game. I prefer the 1 p.m. starts, though, because I get home earlier and get a chance to unwind before going to sleep."

That time likely was spent playing with her dogs. Carrie said, over the past 30 years, she's had several labs, even a black and yellow one, and always decks them out in Steelers-themed collars and leashes. Even though the Steelers have a strong following in the Harrisburg area, according to local newspaper *The Patriot-News*, the NFL has deemed the area to be the Baltimore Ravens home area. That means the Ravens, the Steelers' archrivals ever since they moved from Cleveland for the 1996 season, have their games televised there all the time—the Steelers are only on when they're playing a national game. Carrie even believed that the Philadelphia Eagles had more fans in her area than the Ravens, but the NFL will not budge on this matter right now. So Carrie listens to Steelers road games on their radio network affiliate in Harrisburg when they're not televised and tries to attend every home game.

"I wouldn't miss the Steelers for anything, on the radio, on television, or in person," Carrie said. "I remember way back when they were so bad. You almost couldn't watch them, but I did then—and I'll always watch them."

For Barnes and the Steelers' long-suffering fans, the wait was finally over.

2

WHERE IT ALL STARTED

AFC Divisional Playoff Game
Three Rivers Stadium
Pittsburgh, Pennsylvania
December 23, 1972

LIKE MOST PITTSBURGH-AREA YOUTHS, Ken Scharding was a born-and-raised Steelers fan. When not watching games on television, he attended them when possible with his father at either Pitt Stadium or Forbes Field. And when he began dating his future wife, Barb Pociernicki, she naturally became a Steelers fan as well. As their love fostered their family, so perhaps did their devotion to the Steelers bring them even closer. Ken recalled watching and listening to Steelers games with the entire family, even though the children were too young to know what was going on.

"Ken made sure the kids knew about the Steelers," Barb said. "We had baby books for them where we could write about their first words, the first steps they took, and things like that. But Ken would write something about each Steelers game, too."

The Steelers, long a laughingstock in pro football, gave Scharding little to write about early in his marriage, but that all changed when owner Art Rooney Sr. hired Chuck Noll to coach the club in 1969. The Steelers moved to newly built Three Rivers Stadium in 1970, and things started to improve for the franchise. The Schardings wanted to be part of it and bought season tickets that year. The tickets remain in the family, of course, even after the Steelers moved to Heinz Field 30 years later. The Schardings' four children use the tickets now and rarely miss a game either in person or on television, just as they were raised to do. . . .

Perhaps predestined to do.

Barb might not have known much about football in those early years, but she became a big fan, attending games in 1970 even while she was pregnant with her second child. And even when she was in the hospital for surgery several weeks during the summer of 1977, just a couple months before the season began, Barb still didn't miss the home opener. While the Schardings were taking in the atmosphere during that game, Ken noticed that his wife was crying. After the health scare, she had thought that she might never see another football game with her husband again.

But the two would continue to go to games. None in those early years, however, were as exciting as the 1972 playoff game against the powerful Oakland Raiders. They were a team the Steelers already had beaten in the regular-season opener that year. Yet, this was a playoff game, and the Steelers, to that point, were relative postseason novices.

The club had made just two previous playoff appearances—a 21-0 loss to Philadelphia to snap a tie atop the Eastern Conference in 1947 and a 17-10 loss to Detroit in the playoff bowl (for the league's two second-place teams) after the 1962 season. The winner would finish third in the league.

The Steelers actually appeared to be on the verge of their first playoff victory, but a 6-0 lead turned into a 7-6 deficit when Oakland backup quarterback Ken Stabler scrambled 30 yards for a touchdown with 1:13 remaining. The Steelers got the ball back one final time to win the game.

These were dire straits indeed. The Steelers and their loyal fans were just happy to be in the playoffs. Forty years with few accomplishments will do that to a team and its fan base, and the Steelers' beloved owner—Art Rooney Sr.—left the owner's box for the locker room. He wanted to thank his boys for a great run. The Steelers were 11-3 in just their fourth season under head coach

Chuck Noll, who had led the club to its first winning season since 1963.

But the Schardings remained steadfast and continued to cheer for their team. Everybody was standing, Barb said, and Three Rivers Stadium was rocking like never before. It was a moment that would be difficult to forget—for what happened to that point and what would soon transpire.

Quarterback Terry Bradshaw drove the Steelers from their own 20 to the Raiders' 40, but he faced a fourth-and-10 situation with 22 seconds left. Noll called the 66 Circle Option play, which featured tight end Barry Pearson as the primary target on a deep-post route. As Bradshaw dropped back to pass, though, he was forced to the right hash marks by Oakland defensive end Tony Cline. Bradshaw also had to avoid Raiders lineman Horace Jones before he fired the ball downfield some 40 yards in the direction of running back John "Frenchy" Fuqua. Raiders defensive back Jack Tatum converged. The football, Fuqua, and Tatum simultaneously arrived at the same spot.

"If Terry didn't get flushed from the pocket, he could have hit me with a short pass," Fuqua said. "I could have caught it and then got out of bounds in field-goal range for Roy Gerela. He would have made the chip shot, and we would've won 9-7. But I guess everything happens for a reason."

Tatum played in the secondary, but he hit like a linebacker—a guided missile with a helmet was a more appropriate description—and he lined up Fuqua for an explosive collision. Few got up after a Tatum hit, and he was primed for another violent collision. The Schardings and more than 50,000 frenzied fans waited for this moment. It seemed to last forever.

Even though Three Rivers Stadium was just over two years old, it was the perfect backdrop. In their dubious 40-year history to date, the Steelers and their fans had not experienced anything like this, so they wanted to savor it. It wasn't fair that four decades of futility rested on this one play, but football—like life—isn't always fair. The fate of the franchise hung in the balance.

After compiling just eight winning seasons in the previous 39, the Steelers certainly couldn't go in any direction but up, and they had more seasons of two or fewer victories (10) than they had seasons over .500 (eight). They had three coaches during the 11-game 1941 season and went 1-9-1, then combined with the Philly Eagles to become the Steagles in 1943 and '44. The 1944 group went 0-10.

The Schardings weren't alive for every previous season, but they had seen enough to know this was a big game. No game in the previous seasons was better than this one. It was the playoffs. The city and stadium were alive like never before for a football game. Sure, both played host to a World Series a year earlier, but Western Pennsylvania was a tough, blue-collar area that produced steel by the tons. Those hardhatted fans loved hard-hitting football, and they so badly wanted to embrace the Steelers as their team.

"It was obvious that the game had an amazing effect on Pittsburgh," Barb Scharding said. "Three Rivers Stadium was as alive and as joyous as it had been to that point. You have to remember where we had been. We never won anything up to that point. Nothing that meant anything, that's for sure.

"That season, Ken and I fought over the Monday morning paper to read about Sunday's football games, and we would scream at the television on Monday nights [during *Monday Night Football*]. I did my ironing on Monday nights just to get through the games because [Howard] Cosell drove me crazy."

Monday Night Football was in its infancy back then, as was the Steelers-Raiders rivalry. The teams had played just twice before—a 31-14 Raiders win at Oakland in 1970, and an exciting 34-28 Steelers win at home in the first game of 1972. Since the Raiders had already played in a Super Bowl, the opening win went a long way to legitimize the Steelers during those early stages of Noll's rebuilding process.

A win in this playoff game could do even more for a Steelers franchise that badly needed a boost. Postseason sites rotated by division back then, and it was the AFC Central Division's turn to be the host. Thus, the Steelers received the opening playoff game and, if victorious, secured home-field advantage in the AFC championship as well. This was a chance for Pittsburgh to put on its best face with a nation watching.

However, the NFL did not televise games in the home cities until 1973, so fans had to listen to the radio call of the game or take a short trip to Ohio or West Virginia to watch the national television broadcast. Only 50,327 attended the game, and the Schardings were among them.

Ken and his college roommate at Dayton, Jimmy Puhala, saw their first Steelers game in Noll's inaugural season, 1969. The Steelers beat Detroit that day, 16-13, but lost the final 13 games that season. They had rookie "Mean" Joe Greene to anchor the defense; and with just one win, got to draft No. 1 in 1970 and chose Bradshaw. As Noll rebuilt the team, many fine drafts followed. The prospect of success, as well as the ease with which tickets could be purchased, persuaded Scharding and Puhala to buy season packages.

"Jimmy worked downtown and went over to the Steelers offices," Scharding said. "Their offices were in the Roosevelt Hotel back then, and they would do anything to get season-ticket holders. So, they were thrilled to give us tickets, and at one time, we had nine, I believe."

As friends and relatives who shared the season tickets left town for various reasons, the Schardings kept three tickets. Ken took his wife and father to the playoff game in 1972.

"Barb went to the games with me, and we took Dad as a treat for him," Ken Scharding said, "to a great game against the hated Raiders."

Actually, the Raiders weren't as hated at that time—not yet. An intense dislike, however, quickly grew to hatred from one coast to the other. The two teams would play 20 more times after this playoff game, including five more in the postseason and once at Oakland during the regular season in 2006. The rivalry has waned in recent years, mostly because the Raiders haven't been as competitive in the AFC, but the matchups were as fierce as any in the NFL during the 1970s with future Pro Football Hall of Famers on both sides.

And it all started with the AFC divisional playoff game in 1972—later named the No. 1 NFL game of all time—but it was more than that. The game gave birth to a rivalry that was the league's best for a decade, and it jump-started the Steelers for an amazing run.

"We didn't like them, and they didn't like us," Steelers defensive end Dwight White said. "And we played some great games against each other. But that game in '72, that really got us going. They had some veterans on their team and were among the best teams in the league. Plus, they already played in a Super Bowl. So we felt that if we could beat them, it would elevate our standing in the league."

The major players in that first playoff matchup in 1972—Bradshaw, Franco Harris, Tatum, and Fuqua—tread starkly different paths during their NFL careers. The first three played major roles for their respective teams in the 1970s, while Fuqua was mostly a bit player for the Steelers from 1970-76. Bradshaw and Fuqua were just in their third NFL seasons, while Tatum was in his second. And Harris was a rookie.

Bradshaw (twice) and Harris were Super Bowl MVPs and elected to the Pro Football Hall of Fame on their first ballots. Tatum's NFL legacy is more dubious. While he was a three-time Pro Bowl performer (1973-75), "The Assassin," as Tatum was called, was known more for his dirty hits than good plays. His most notable came against New England wideout Darryl Stingley, a hit that permanently paralyzed the receiver in 1978.

Before that, though, was the hit on Fuqua in 1972.

Fuqua had led the Steelers in rushing his first two seasons—691 yards and seven touchdowns as a rookie and 625 with four scores in 1971—but he was supplanted as the top back by a No. 1 pick named Harris from Penn State in 1972. Fuqua was a solid running back during his Steelers tenure, but he was better known for his off-field antics. Fuqua was a flashy dresser who combined various hats and capes with bright-colored outfits. His most famous shoes had big, clear heels that he filled with water and live goldfish. His most noted on-field moment, however, came against the Raiders in that 1972 playoff game.

"[Bradshaw] should've been able to hit Pearson, who was wide open [on a pass route]," Fuqua remembered. "But I looked directly into [Bradshaw's] blue eyes, and I knew he was going to throw to me.

"I could see Tatum was heading toward the middle of the field, and that the location of the pass would bring me on a collision

As a rookie, Franco Harris made one of the most famous catches in NFL history, the "Immaculate Reception."

course with him. I was thinking, 'I just want to get my body between him and the ball.' As Bradshaw released the ball, and there was Tatum. I heard his footsteps, then I heard his breath; and then, his heartbeat."

As Tatum and Fuqua collided, the ball catapulted backward. Harris, who initially stayed close to block for Bradshaw, had slowly drifted downfield. He quickly picked up speed and caught the ball at his shoe tops around the 42-yard line, then raced down the sideline into the end zone.

"I remember, after I made that hit, we all thought the game was over," Tatum said. "I saw Franco Harris running and thought, 'Man, that guy's in a hurry to get to the locker room.' We thought we had that game won."

But nobody knew for sure what had happened.

"The ball hit Tatum or Frenchy, I don't know, and it bounced way up in the air," Ken Scharding said. "That's when I turned to my Dad and said, 'Same Old Steelers.' SOS, that was the saying back then. But I heard the crowd roar, and Barb started hitting me on the arm.

"I didn't see him catch it, but I saw Franco running down the far sideline toward the goal line. I wasn't sure what happened, but it sure sounded good. And, as it turns out, he caught the ball out of the air and scored the winning touchdown. The place went wild. It was bonkers; and we had seen the play that later became known as the 'Immaculate Reception.'"

But no one was certain about anything at that point.

"All the fans were standing, and it was somewhat hard to see," Barb Scharding said. "There was a lot of noise, and everybody was carrying on because the game was almost over. I just remember watching, and Franco ended up with the ball. Ken wasn't watching at that point. I hit him on the shoulder and asked him, 'What's it all mean?'

"There was so much chaos in the stands that I didn't really know what was going on. I wasn't sure what exactly happened, and I certainly wasn't sure what it all meant. Did we get the ball? Was the game over? Did we win the game? I guess nobody knew for sure until they figured it all out."

The Raiders argued that Fuqua touched the ball, and NFL rules at that time did not permit consecutive touches by offensive players. If the officials ruled that Tatum batted the ball, it would be a touchdown. Referee Fred Swearingen, after consulting with NFL supervisor of officials Art McNally, came back on the field and ruled the play a touchdown. The Steelers kicked the extra point to take a 13-7 lead. That score became final moments later, instantaneously ending four decades of futility for the Steelers. It was the first of many playoff wins, and it fueled the NFL's most heated rivalry in the 1970s.

Steelers defensive end L.C. Greenwood never saw the play.

"I was talking to the man upstairs," Greenwood said. "I didn't want to interrupt what I was doing. Next thing I know, the guys were jumping around, and there went Franco. I just said: 'Lord, I hope he has the ball.' He did."

Noll said that Harris was rewarded for mere hustle.

"Franco made that [great catch] because he never quit on the play," Noll said. "He kept running. ... Good things happen to those who [do that]."

Ken and Barb Scharding show off their Steelers spirit.

Bradshaw didn't know what to think about the improbable play, but he knew it probably would always be one of a kind.

"I've played football since the second grade, and nothing like that had ever happened," Bradshaw said. "It'll never happen again."

Tatum has maintained that he never touched the ball. He only drilled Fuqua. Raiders coach John Madden blamed it on the flight from Oakland. "We got fogged in [at the airport] at the start of the trip, and nothing went right from then on," Madden said.

Yet, the fog that had engulfed the Steelers for 40 years was lifted by this win. Same Old Steelers? Not any more. When he went on the air that night, Myron Cope dubbed Harris' catch as the "Immaculate Reception." A fan suggested the name to him just before his broadcast—and it's now the most famous NFL play of all time.

A week after the win against Oakland, the Steelers lost to the Miami Dolphins—who went on to win the Super Bowl to complete their perfect 17-0 season—but the Steelers were primed for future success. The sad '60s had become the Super '70s with a single play, and the Steelers earned Team of the Decade honors. Bradshaw and Harris were prominent in all four Super Bowl wins.

Fuqua played in two, but he forever would be remembered for his role in the play that turned the team's fortunes. Only he knows for sure what really happened on the play. Was divine intervention present? We may never know. The late Art Rooney Sr., Fuqua has said, told him to "let it stay immaculate." And Fuqua, a product manager for a Detroit newspaper, hasn't come clean to this day. Maybe, someday, Fuqua will break his silence, revealing a secret that has remained unknown for three-plus decades. No matter, history will mark that day as a turning point for the Steelers.

"Everybody knew it was just a matter of time when Chuck [Noll] took over," Barb Scharding said. "You could just sense it, especially on that day; and it's something I'll always remember. I'm very glad I was there, even though I didn't exactly know what I had seen or what it all meant. I was glad to be there, thrilled to be a part of it. It was very special."

Barb Scharding met up with Harris more than three decades later in a Pittsburgh-area mall, but felt apprehensive, initially, in approaching him. After sending her daughter, Denise, ahead to ask for an autograph, Barb Scharding rushed up to Harris and told him she saw him make the "Immaculate Reception."

"That was a long time ago," Harris replied.

Yet, for the Schardings and those Steelers fans who saw the play live—along with those who only wish they were there—it will never be forgotten.

3

WELL WORTH THE JOURNEY

AFC Championship Game
Oakland Alameda County Coliseum
Oakland, California
December 29, 1974

AT FIRST GLANCE, Gordon Dedman's website doesn't appear as if it would be too appealing to Pittsburgh Steelers fans. Honest mistakes could be made, and www.steelersuk.com has been mistaken for an abbreviated "Steelers suck." A closer read reveals that the address actually represents "Steelers UK." Dedman, you see, lives in the United Kingdom; and, when it comes to the Steelers, he's as serious as any Pittsburgh native.

"The Steelers are a great team," Dedman said. "American football, it's provided me with a lot of superb moments in my life. And following the Steelers has been a wonderful experience."

One might wonder how Dedman, 59, became a devout Steelers fan despite the 3,500-mile gap between his hometown of Fareham—located on the South Coast of England near Portsmouth Naval Base—and Pittsburgh. Like many Steelers fans, Dedman became enamored with the club while watching games from the 1970s teams that won four Super Bowls in a six-season span from 1974 to 1979.

Yet, Dedman never actually *watched* a game until a few years later, and he mostly saw mere bits and pieces from Steelers games in that era because American football wasn't telecast in the United Kingdom until 1981. Even then, Dedman could only see 20-minute highlights from Super Bowls.

"I remember vague pictures from those early years, but I enjoyed it," Dedman said. "I always had an interest in America, mostly through politics; and I was brought up around John and Robert Kennedy's time. So, I already had an interest in America and decided to have a look at American football.

"But I have to be committed. I can't just sit down and watch any sporting event without wanting one side to win or the other to lose, so I decided to follow a specific team. While deciding, I remembered the old highlights and a team in black and gold. So I started to follow the Steelers. I missed the good years, I guess, but they got better eventually."

Even though he didn't really begin following the Steelers until after the heroes from those 1970s Super Bowl years were retired and had to endure the Bubby Brister-led club that finished just 5-11 in 1988, Dedman's interest in the club never waned. In fact, he soon joined a fan club in the United Kingdom and eventually took it over when the president left. Dedman quickly found out that the Steelers fans in the UK club were just like him. They too remembered those original American football highlights, primarily with the Super Bowl Champion Steelers being featured, and decided to cheer for them.

Dedman noted that, while there aren't that many fans in the UK club right now—maybe a dozen or so—around 100 members were in the club six or seven years ago. Back then, Dedman produced a newsletter on a regular basis to inform members about various club activities and Steelers news and notes; but he couldn't continue that after his wife, Carol, became ill and later passed away. While the newsletter was never rekindled, Dedman maintains the website and updates it with Steelers information as often as possible. To illustrate how far-reaching the site is, as well as the Steelers' power in the UK, has become, Dedman relayed a story about a man from the Shetlands, some "hundreds and hundreds of miles away," who was visiting in his area and looked him up.

Steelers fan Gordon Dedman (left), who lives in England, seeks an autograph from Pittsburgh quarterback Ben Roethlisberger.

NFL fans in the United Kingdom have it much better today since more games are televised. Dedman said they get two games every Sunday night, including the late game on a different channel; and, of course, every Monday night game, and odd-day games like Thursdays or Saturdays late in the season, is aired. The UK also gets the Thanksgiving Day games. Yet, while the United States is watching a multitude of matchups on any given Sunday, Dedman noted, he only gets to see two games for sure, possibly three, on Sundays during the season. Keep in mind that Dedman lives in a time zone that is five hours later than the East Coast.

"We didn't get many Steelers games on television for a while there, but this year (2006) has been brilliant," Dedman said. "As the reigning Super Bowl champs, we've had more Steelers games than in any other season. You might get lucky enough to see them on a Sunday, but the producer of the satellite program thought they should show the Steelers a lot."

Dedman also has an NFL Field Pass membership; so he can listen to Steelers games on the Internet through the team website, allowing him to listen to any Steelers games that aren't aired on TV. But Dedman doesn't limit following the Steelers to television and radio broadcasts. He has scheduled trips to Pittsburgh to watch the club and has seen them play preseason games against the San Francisco 49ers in Barcelona, Spain (1995) and against the Chicago Bears in Dublin, Ireland (1997). Dedman's first organized trip to Pittsburgh came in 1993, when the Steelers were playing Cleveland, an opponent he will go out of his way to see.

Dedman has developed some friendships in the organization as well, including chief photographer Mike Fabus and former radio commentator Myron Cope. Dedman first met Cope at the game in Barcelona, and he later met him in Pittsburgh and was a special guest on his radio talk show. "I really love the guy," Dedman said. "I know a lot of fans say that, but he was very friendly and helpful from the moment I met him; and he really didn't know me from Adam at the time."

Dedman contacted Dan Edwards from the Steelers media relations department to determine where the team was staying and later called the hotel to speak with Cope. The desk rang his room, and Dedman told him there were about a dozen English Steelers fans in town who wanted to meet him. Cope invited the group to visit the hotel; and when they arrived, he quickly left to find Steelers coach Bill Cowher to arrange a meeting. Though Cowher had left for the evening, they still had a great time with Cope.

Dedman's daughter, Jodie, who was 21 at the time, arranged a trip to Pittsburgh for her father's 50th birthday. The Steelers played the Denver Broncos on December 7, 1997, a game they won 35–24, but also lost to the Broncos in the AFC championship game later that season. While that initial victory enriched the Dedman family trip to Pittsburgh, Mike Fabus also arranged for them to visit Three Rivers Stadium for a tour and lunch with some Steelers players. Jodie quite fondly remembered meeting former Steelers linebacker Levon Kirkland, and it was the best birthday present Dedman had ever received.

Along with his wife and daughter, Dedman has seen some 20 Steelers games in person over the years. Dedman went alone more often than not, but that wasn't the extent of his involvement with American football, as he called it. He also learned the game's rules and ran the chains for a game or two.

"When I run into people who don't watch the NFL on television here, I think it's because they don't understand the rules," Dedman said. "I was very fortunate, though, because when I first saw American football on TV here, there was a players' strike. The TV company had no recent games to show, so they had a lot of time to teach us the rules, which was what we needed."

Dedman was soon able to learn what American Football was all about, and he ended up officiating games in the United Kingdom, which he did for 15 years before recently retiring. He said that he had to pass a written test every year to be certified. Fans and English coaches used to abuse the referees, Dedman noted; but he believed it was just because they didn't understand the rules as well as the officials. Even the American coaches gave them a hard time; probably because they believed they knew more than the officials, Dedman surmised.

Even though he was harassed occasionally, Dedman was not deterred. He ran the chains for the London Monarchs in NFL Europe and for an NFL preseason game between the Los Angeles Rams and Denver Broncos—with quarterback John Elway—at Wembley Stadium. Names were pulled from a hat to select the English officials in the area who knew the rules since the NFL didn't send their own chains crews.

Those experiences have made Dedman among the more knowledgeable Steelers fans in the United Kingdom, but that doesn't get him better seats when he comes to Pittsburgh for games. It has, however, helped develop relationships with other fans in the area. He became friends with Sherri Caplan from Carnegie and Ed and Jodi Beeler from Moon Township, who Dedman met through eBay. He bought a Steelers media guide from Beeler and even attended Super Bowl XL with him—a cherished memory. After myriad attempts to secure a ticket to see Pittsburgh capture its fifth Super Bowl title, the journey was well worth the time and expenses.

The Steelers had hoped the same would ring true as they made their first jaunt across the United States to play for the AFC championship in 1974. The Oakland Raiders, the team that had been party to the "Immaculate Reception" in 1972, awaited them. Though the Raiders had hammered Pittsburgh 33-14 in their 1973 AFC wild-card playoff matchup, the Steelers had won at Oakland just six weeks prior to the '74 conference title game.

A serious rivalry was brewing.

Since Chuck Noll had become the Steelers' head coach in 1969, the Steelers and Raiders had played only a handful of times to this point. The Steelers lost at Oakland in 1970 (31-14), didn't play in 1971, opened 1972 with a 34-28 win against the Raiders at Three Rivers Stadium and later beat them there again in an AFC Divisional playoff game that same year. The two 1973 games set the stage for changes to the Steelers in 1974. "Jefferson Street" Joe Gilliam, an African-American quarterback with a strong arm and a gunslinger mentality, guided the Steelers offense instead of Terry Bradshaw. The Steelers opened with a 30-0 blowout win against the Baltimore Colts, a 35-35 tie against the Denver Broncos in the NFL's first overtime regular-season game and a 17-0 loss to the Raiders before they turned things around to begin a run to the playoffs. The Steelers went 9-2 after that 1-1-1 start and pummeled the Buffalo Bills 32-14 in an AFC Divisional playoff game to set up the game at Oakland for the AFC championship.

"We had a chance to get back in the playoffs in 1973, and the Oakland Raiders beat our butts out there," Steelers veteran outside linebacker Andy Russell said. "So we didn't want that to happen again in 1974, but we really didn't know if we could get by Oakland. It was a difficult challenge. So to go out there in '74, nobody thought we could win. We had won a division title in 1972 and won the playoff game against the Raiders on Franco's catch. Then we lost to a team that we were better than, the Miami Dolphins, because we played the wrong defense. The rest of the time, we never played that defense again, and we killed them. We wanted to turn things around against the Raiders in 1974 as well."

Even though the Steelers were on a roll, that wouldn't be easy because the Raiders were favored at home and already had beaten the two-time Super Bowl champion Dolphins the previous week—

a wild 28-26 win on quarterback Ken Stabler's last-second touchdown pass to Clarence Davis. After that dynamic victory, Oakland coach John Madden said it was great that the two best NFL teams could play such a great game. Others labeled the matchup the real Super Bowl. All those comments angered Noll and the Steelers, Russell said, and it prompted Noll to make one of his more impassioned pregame speeches. The story goes that Noll, who did not believe he needed to motivate his players with Knute Rockne-like talks, said that Madden and all those other naysayers could believe what they wanted. He knew the best team in the NFL was the one in that locker room.

"Most observers figured the Raiders were ready to take the crown from the Dolphins and establish their own dynasty," Russell explained. "Plus, we were tagged with the reputation of not being winners—even though we had made it to the 1972 AFC Championship Game before losing to the Dolphins."

"We were determined to win this one," Steelers outside linebacker Jack Ham said. "For me, every team's goal is to get to the championship; so, in some ways, this game would be more important than the Super Bowl. This is the game we'd been pointing to since the first day of training camp."

Another legendary pregame story has Steelers defensive end L.C. Greenwood watching the NFC championship game on television in the tunnel to the field. When asked by Raiders players what he was doing, Greenwood calmly responded that he wanted to see which team the Steelers were going to face in the upcoming Super Bowl. That's how confident the Steelers were going into the game, and it was a battle from the outset, as the Raiders scored first with a 40-yard field goal by George Blanda. The Steelers tied the score in the second quarter on Roy Gerela's 23-yard field goal, but the Raiders regained their advantage in the third when Stabler found speedy wideout Cliff Branch with a 38-yard pass and catch for a touchdown. Branch would haul in nine Stabler tosses for 186 yards with the one big touchdown.

However, the Steelers held the high-powered Oakland ground attack to just 24 yards rushing, including a team-high 16 on 10 carries by tailback Clarence Davis, forcing Stabler to the air. While the usually accurate quarterback had some success, the Steelers actually had the Raiders right where they wanted them. They picked off Stabler three times with two coming in the final 10 minutes in a crucial fourth quarter.

"We had pressured Stabler all day, and they just couldn't run on us," Steelers defensive end Dwight White said. "But their defense did a good job, too; and our offense didn't break through until the fourth quarter."

A long Steelers drive comprised the final minutes of the third and opening seconds into the fourth. Harris capped the drive by blasting into the end zone from eight yards out to tie the score at 10-10. The Raiders wanted to put the game away, so Stabler came out throwing on the ensuing possession, but the Steelers' "Steel Curtain" defense came down hard. Safety Glen Edwards blitzed Stabler to force a wobbly pass to Charlie Smith, and Ham stepped in front and picked it off along the Oakland sideline. Ham ran it back to inside the 10-yard line. A few plays later, Steelers quarterback Terry Bradshaw connected with wideout Lynn Swann for a six-yard score. Gerela's conversion kick gave the Steelers a 17-10 advantage. Stabler marched the Raiders back down the field on their ensuing possession and got deep in Steelers territory, but on third down at the 12, he fired an incomplete pass to force a field goal. Blanda made the 24-yard chip shot to get within four points, 17-13, and the Raiders were back in the game.

The Steelers couldn't move the sticks in the remaining minutes, so Stabler and the Raiders had one last chance to drive on the Steelers defense for the winning score. The Steel Curtain, however, wouldn't make it easy. From their secondary and linebacking spots, the Steelers were blitzing on just about every down, while the defensive line was hammering Oakland's offensive front. Stabler tried to remain cool as he dropped back to pass and fired the ball downfield into the Steelers secondary. Yet, his pass was picked off by cornerback J.T. Thomas and returned deep into Raiders territory. Just a few plays later, Harris ripped off a 21-yard scoring run to seal the Steelers' first AFC title and a spot in Super Bowl IX. Oakland, however, had lost its fifth straight championship game.

"This game was a defining moment for us," Russell said. "I think it was the quintessential game for the Steelers franchise, the biggest game in their history. If we win the game, we go to the Super Bowl for the first time, and that was huge. But if we lost, I think it could have crushed us. We probably would have been known as the good team that never won the big game."

Russell noted that, in 1963, when there were 12 teams in the NFL—six in the East and six in the West—the Steelers played the final game against the New York Giants at Yankee Stadium. They already beat the Giants 31-0 at Forbes Field, but New York quarterback Y.A. Tittle—a future Hall of Famer—did not play in that game. Russell said that the old veterans on the Steelers, like defensive tackle Ernie Stautner, still believed they could beat the Giants again. But they lost, 33-17, to end their title hopes. A win would have forced a second matchup against the powerful Chicago Bears in the NFL championship game. The Steelers had tied the Bears several weeks earlier at Forbes Field, but Russell said the club should have won that game. Steelers running back Dick Hoak broke off a long run for a touchdown, but it was called back; and the score ended in a 17-17 tie.

"We thought it was just (Bears coach) George Halas pulling some (crap)," Russell said. "So, we were that close to a championship in 1963, but we had to wait all those years to get back for another shot in 1974, more than a decade. It was a very long time for some of us."

The long wait ended that afternoon in Oakland, but for the Steelers, it was well worth the journey.

4

LET THE
DYNASTY BEGIN

Super Bowl IX
Tulane Stadium
New Orleans, Louisiana
January 12, 1975

LIKE MANY PITTSBURGH STEELERS FANS, Harvey
Aronson eats, sleeps, and drinks everything concerning the
Pittsburgh Steelers 24 hours a day and seven days a week during each
NFL season, but he certainly doesn't take a break during the off-
season. He's consumed by the Steelers then.

But Aronson isn't an ordinary Steelers fan by any means. In fact,
he's come to be known as "Mr. Steeler." Though he didn't come by
that moniker easily, he certainly doesn't take the title lightly, either.

Aronson grew up in Pittsburgh's North Hills area, but he now
lives in Jacksonville, Florida, and helps run that area's Steelers fan
club. He also handles several websites dealing with the Steelers and
is a past winner of the Visa Hall of Fans Award for the Steelers.
Aronson was inducted into the Pro Football Hall of Fame in 2002,
where a plaque commemorates the award.

"I live for the Steelers, 24-7, that's for sure," Aronson said. "People
know that about me. . . . There's a guy at Steelers games with a black-
and-gold car who's called 'The ultimate Steelers Fan.' I sat on that car
and got a photo taken to submit. He won the fan award for the
Steelers in 2000, and that photo helped me win it the following year."

Aronson attended the Hall of Fame ceremony with his favorite Steelers cap and jersey, but was astonished to see the other NFL team winners. Among the fans in attendance were the Cleveland Browns' Big Dawg, the Hogettes from the Washington Redskins, Captain Defense from the Baltimore Ravens, the Philadelphia Eagles' Bird Man, and Panther Man from the Carolina Panthers. With those guys in full team costume, Aronson felt a little bit underdressed and not as representative.

So, after that experience, Aronson created his own dynamic Steelers black-and-gold outfit complete with a bright yellow jacket, pants, and a hat to wear to the ceremony the following year. He wears it to Steelers games and events like reunions with other Hall of Fans winners and received the nickname Mr. Steeler just a short time after designing the outfit.

On one such occasion, at the 2003 NFL Draft in New York City, Aronson and other top fans were in full costume when *Sports Illustrated* photographers began filming the event. When they came upon Aronson, he blurted, "Go Steelers." He and Philly's Bird Man ended up in a *Sports Illustrated* commercial a short time later that ran for a year. A photo depicting Aronson's TV stint graces his websites.

Aronson is owner and editor of www.steelershotline.com, vice-president and director of operations for Jacksonville Black and Gold—Jacksonville's official Pittsburgh Steelers Fan Club at jaxbag.steelershotline.com—and the Southeast Representative for Steelers Fans United at snu.steelershotline.com.

Aronson has a background in desktop publishing, creative work with graphics and publication design, and he has a new job with an engineering company in Jacksonville. But he spends a great deal of time on the Steelers websites that are viewed by some 600 fans on a regular basis and many other casual browsers. Aronson's wife, Melba, and 21-year-old stepdaughter, Meaghan, aren't really interested in the Steelers—certainly not as much as Aronson and his friends, even though he forewarned her—but that doesn't deter him.

If somebody says or writes something derogatory about the Steelers, Aronson really takes it personally. Since he has access to a multitude of fans through the internet, he can be extremely persuasive.

"There was this guy from Fox, it was amazing," Aronson said. "I really got after him. I gave his e-mail address out to all our Steelers fans, and they bombarded him to tell him where he made a mistake. He got so many e-mails that he was forced to apologize. To have that power, that was great."

In his role with the Steelers fan club in Jacksonville, he helped organize a pep rally and party before the team's *Monday Night Football* matchup against the Jaguars September 18, 2006. Aronson warned the owner of their weekly game-time hangout that there would be an overflow crowd for the party, so additional waitstaff and supplies would be needed. Aronson believed about 300 Steelers fans would attend the event, but the Steelers Nation came out in full force for this one. And Aronson badly underestimated how strongly the Steelers would be represented.

"People were everywhere," Aronson said. "We ended up having from 800 to 1,000 people there. The party overflowed into the parking lot."

Of course, Aronson wore his Mr. Steeler outfit for the event, which included such notables as former Pittsburgh Pirates pitcher and commentator Jim Rooker and the daughter of former Steelers Super Bowl coach Bud Carson, who now lives in Jacksonville. It was a huge bash, but that wasn't the extent of it. The NFL Network showed up to film the event for an NFL fan documentary that aired later in the season.

Aronson has since found a new establishment to spend Sunday afternoons during football season, and the Steelers Fan Club in Jacksonville is thriving. Since he got involved with it three years ago, the club's membership more than tripled from about 75 to 80 members to 250-plus fans—and it can only grow from there.

Similarly, the Steelers fortunes were cultivated when University of Dayton graduate Charles Henry Noll, a former messenger guard with the Cleveland Browns, was chosen to be the team's head coach in 1969. The Steelers finished 2-11-1 in 1968 in Bill Austin's third and final season as the head coach, but they couldn't even match that in Noll's first, finishing 1-13 with a lengthy losing streak after winning the opener.

Steelers safety Mike Wagner noted that Noll and his coaching staff put forth a message that the losing was over, and a winning team would be put onto the field. To Steelers such as Wagner, a low-round draft pick in 1971, it quickly became evident that the club was as good if not better than any other team in the league. The coaches just had to get the players to believe in themselves and work hard to accomplish that goal.

All that paid off when the Steelers arrived in New Orleans to face the Minnesota Vikings in Super Bowl IX at Tulane Stadium. After going 10-3-1 in the regular season, in which they rebounded after a 1-1-1 start and whipped Buffalo in the first playoff round 32-14, they also dispatched Oakland 24-13 in the AFC championship game to get a shot at the Vikings in the Super Bowl. But the Steelers were dealt a huge blow when defensive end Dwight White had to be rushed to the hospital Sunday night, a short time after the team arrived, due to abdominal pain. The big game was less than six days away.

"Joe Greene, L.C. Greenwood, and I, we went down to the French quarter to get something to eat shortly after we arrived in New Orleans," White said. "All of a sudden, I got this pain, and it got progressively worse. It was so painful that I couldn't breathe."

White's two defensive linemates stuffed their teammate in a cab and sent him back to the Steelers hotel where he could be looked at by the team's doctor. White was in excruciating pain, doubled over in the fetal position "even though I was standing up." So White quickly was admitted to a local hospital. He was diagnosed with having a viral pneumonia and pleurisy, an infection of the pleural lining in his lungs. So every time White's lungs expanded, it was quite painful. He apparently left Pittsburgh with the infection, although White believed he just had a bad cold.

White had to have breathing solutions administered to decrease the infections and clean out his lungs. And since he didn't eat anything for several days he lost some 20 pounds. White stayed in the hospital from that Sunday night through Thursday—four nights—but he expected to practice that day since he was feeling better. White went through a brief workout but had to be rushed back to

GEORGE GOJKOVICH/GETTY IMAGES

Dwight White left the hospital and put on a dominant performance for the Steelers in Super Bowl IX.

the hospital. He stayed until Sunday morning, game day, and he wanted to play even though he didn't appear well.

"Chuck and Bud (defensive coordinator Carson) believed I would just conk out in warmups," White said. "I made it through, and Chuck said I could start the game. They still thought I would drop at any minute, but I played the whole game; and I think I played pretty well."

White and the Steelers "Steel Curtain" defense dominated the Vikings from the outset, but Minnesota's "Purple People Eaters" defense was solid as well. There was no score throughout the first quarter and midway through the second, as Minnesota place-kicker Fred Cox missed a 39-yard field goal. But the Steelers finally scored a safety when Vikings quarterback Fran Tarkenton's weak pitch to running back Dave Osborn was mishandled. White tackled Tarkenton in the end zone to record the first safety in Super Bowl history. The Steelers forced another fumble later in the half, when safety Glen Edwards drilled wideout John Gilliam after a catch at the 5. So, instead of first-and-goal, the Steelers had the ball. Wagner, cornerback Mel Blount, and Greene each picked off Tarkenton, and the Steelers held star running back Chuck Foreman to 18 rushing yards. His Vikings teammates managed -1 rushing yards, so Minnesota was held to a Super Bowl-record low of 17 total rushing yards.

The Steelers hammered the Vikings defense in the second half and finally broke through in the third quarter with their running game. Franco Harris, who would run for a then-record 158 rushing yards, ripped off a 24-yard run and then blasted into the end zone from nine yards out. Rocky Bleier added 65 rushing yards to keep Minnesota off-balance. The Steelers offense owed its success, in part at least, to equipment manager Tony Parisi. The transplanted Canadian checked pregame weather conditions and determined that the field could be slick due to heavy rain showers in the days before the game. So the Steelers needed a new shoe to deal with possible problems with poor field conditions.

"I remembered reading something about shoes that had not yet come on the market," Parisi said. "I did a little checking and found I could get this special type of shoe in Montreal, an Acton shoe. I phoned and ordered 75 pairs that arrived a few days before the game. It was a multicleated shoe with spirals on every cleat.

"So when you compressed it onto the ground, it grabbed. It wasn't a hard material, so you were able to get good traction. The bottoms were like spirals. When you're on grass, you in-bed, but on turf you don't. So they gave a little bit and had good traction. I didn't tell the players what to wear, though; I only suggested it."

The Vikings finally got back in the game in the fourth quarter when Matt Blair blocked a Bobby Walden punt deep in Steelers territory, and defensive back Terry Brown recovered the ball in the end zone for a touchdown. Yet Minnesota missed the extra point, so the Steelers still led 9-6 into the fourth quarter.

COURTESY OF HARVEY ARONSON

Harvey Aronson, aka Mr. Steeler, shows off his
Terrible Towel at the Pro Football Hall of Fame.

The game was exciting for all Steelers fans, but Aronson couldn't get too fired up. He had surgery the day before and needed bed rest.

"I was about 15 years old and wasn't too big, so I went crazy lifting weights for seven days a week," Aronson said. "I suffered a hernia and needed surgery. I just remember my dad telling me not to jump up and down and get too excited, or I'd rip my stitches out. I had to watch the Super Bowl from a wheelchair. Fortunately, even though it was close, it was a defensive battle the whole way. Not too much action."

But things picked up for the Steelers in the fourth quarter. More than 10 minutes remained in the game, but quarterback Terry Bradshaw directed a spectacular Steelers drive from their 34 to the Minnesota 4 that lasted nearly seven minutes and featured three consecutive third-down conversions. The first was a clutch 30-yard pass to Larry Brown. It was a key play in the game, because Brown fumbled, but the officials eventually said that the Steelers retained possession since Brown was down by contact. Bradshaw connected with Bleier on another third-down conversion to the 5. But two more plays netted just one yard, so Bradshaw dropped back to pass on third down.

This was Minnesota's third Super Bowl appearance—its second straight after a loss to the Miami Dolphins the previous year—so the Vikings did not want to lose a second straight season and for the third time in nine years. The Steelers, of course, were making their first trip to the NFL's biggest stage after four-plus decades of lackluster play. But it took a lot of hard work to get to this point. Noll's first draft yielded future Hall of Famer Joe Greene, who would anchor the club's defensive front line for more than a decade, in the first round. They also picked offensive tackle Jon Kolb in the third round that year, and he became a stalwart as well.

The Steelers still had cerebral outside linebacker Andy Russell, a late-round pick from the 1963 draft, but a few holdovers remained when Noll took over. Running back Paul Martha, the No. 1 pick in 1964, and second-round wideout Roy Jefferson from 1965 were two notable players who ended their Steelers careers in 1969. Along with Russell (drafted in 1963), the only players from the pre-Noll years to survive into the 1974 season were center Ray Mansfield (1964), offensive guard Sam Davis (1967), punter Bobby Walden, and Rocky Bleier (each in 1968). All four players were starters for the Steelers in 1974, and all but Davis started against the Vikings in the Super Bowl.

"Noll told the players in no uncertain terms that some of them wouldn't be there after his first season," longtime Steelers commentator Myron Cope said, echoing Russell's comments. "The Steelers had been bad for so long and traded away so many draft picks that Noll vowed to start bringing in good players by the draft. So that's what he did from the very beginning."

The Steelers' poor 1969 record secured the No. 1 overall pick in the 1970 draft, where they chose future Hall of Famer Terry Bradshaw, who had a rough start to his career but eventually developed into the big-play quarterback that Noll had envisioned.

They also picked cornerback Mel Blount, another future Hall of Famer, in the third round that year.

The club went 5-9 in 1970 and had a big 1971 draft to go with a 6-8 record. Penn State outside linebacker Jack Ham was the second-round pick in 1971, and Nittany Lions teammate Franco Harris was the No. 1 pick in 1972. Both were future Hall of Famers. The Steelers also picked offensive guard Gerry Mullins, defensive end Dwight White, offensive tackle-tight end Larry Brown, defensive tackle Ernie Holmes, and Wagner in 1971. And offensive lineman Gordon Gravelle, defensive tackle Steve Furness, and quarterback "Jefferson Street" Joe Gilliam were taken in 1972. Defensive back J.T. Thomas was the No. 1 pick in 1973, while linebacker Loren Toews was a late-round selection.

The Steelers followed that somewhat weaker draft with a proverbial touchdown in 1974. Wideout Lynn Swann was the No. 1 pick, and middle linebacker Jack Lambert went in the second round. Wideout John Stallworth was the fourth-round pick, and center Mike Webster came along in the fifth. All four would be elected to the Pro Football Hall of Fame after their retirement and were integral parts of the Steelers Super Bowl teams.

"Not at all to diminish what those players accomplished from the 1974 draft, but coming out of 1972, I think that Noll had put the organization, the team, and the players' confidence over the hump," said Mike Wagner. "It was just a matter of how good could we be? And the nucleus of that 1974 team . . . those players made many contributions.

"But I think that if you'll look at the roster right through that 1974 season, those future Hall of Famers from that team made most of their contributions following 1975 and in later years. I came in 1971 and was part of that losing legacy and attitude and just saw it turn. To me, that's really all that it was. But we really turned things around."

That turnaround would be completed in Super Bowl IX. Each time Bradshaw dropped back to pass, the Steelers' offensive line kept the Vikings out of the pocket and provided enough protection for the wide receivers to spread the defense in the end zone. But instead of hooking up with one of them, Bradshaw found seldom-used tight end Larry Brown in the back near the end line for a touchdown with just 3:38 remaining.

Minnesota had good field position to begin the ensuing drive, but Wagner picked off Tarkenton to seal the victory, and the Steelers began celebrating their first Super Bowl title. Brown was a solid blocker and later became an offensive tackle. He was a stalwart on the offensive line for the Steelers' other three Super Bowl teams in the 1970s. Brown had 17 catches and just one touchdown in the regular season for the Steelers, but his big third-down catch and end-zone reception in Super Bowl IX would be the most critical of his career. In the Super Bowl, role players can make all the difference.

Then there's Dwight White, who was a major contributor during the regular season and would have been sorely missed. He anchored an end position on the Steelers' defensive line and just couldn't miss the biggest game to that point in his young NFL career. He had come way too far.

"You play a whole season, and you're in the Super Bowl," White said. "I didn't want to miss it. I don't think it was anything heroic that I did. That was my spot, and I was responsible for it. So I went out there and did, I think, what any other player would have done. You know, God takes care of fools and babies—and I wasn't a baby."

When the Steelers returned to their team hotel for the post-Super Bowl celebration, all White wanted to do was get something to eat. He didn't have much all week, so he grabbed a cheeseburger and scarfed it down at a sandwich shop across the street and then quickly returned to his hotel room to get a good night's sleep. As soon as the Steelers returned to Pittsburgh, though, White was admitted to Divine Providence Hospital for another week. But if you believe that's the end of White's Super Bowl IX story, you would be wrong. White believed he had been slighted by the NFL.

Since he was in the hospital on the Monday before the game, he wasn't available for the official team photo at the Super Bowl. That was no one's fault, but when the team photo was released, White's name wasn't on it either. Though added later, White felt it was an afterthought, which wasn't good enough.

"It's just like I was never on the football team," White said. "That really bothered me and hurt me, and I had scored the first points in the game. I was pissed off about that for a long time. . . . I guess it was total incompetence, really, but I guess what happened during the game is more important.

"At least I got the ring, but I would have liked to be in the team picture. And at least mention that the poor guy was in the hospital trying to breathe, and he lost 20 pounds. We don't know if he'll live, but . . . oh, well, that was a long time ago. And at least we got the rings."

White said that the Steelers believed they were the better team going into the Super Bowl against the Vikings and the other three, for that matter, because along with a serious group of characters the Steelers also had a solid core group with great character. And that's what it took to be successful in the NFL. They had a good time, but they also had the talent to crank up their play to a higher level at any moment. White gave Noll high marks for getting the Steelers to play together, stay focused, and believe they could be victorious against any opponent.

"We had the talent, so he didn't need to be a teacher as much as a motivator," White added. "And when we had our backs up against the wall, we were even tougher. We were really tough to beat then."

And their defense was impenetrable against the Vikings. To this day, Minnesota is the only Super Bowl team to not score a touchdown or field goal against the opposing team's defense or get a defensive touchdown. The Vikings' only points came off a special-teams play, and they had just nine first downs and 119 yards in total offense against the Steelers.

When the victorious Steelers poured into their surprisingly subdued clubhouse, they found beloved owner 73-year-old Art Rooney Sr. waiting for them. The "Chief," as the team's patriarch was known, wanted to be the first to congratulate his boys. Team captain Andy Russell presented the game ball and later the Vince Lombardi Trophy to a humbled Rooney.

"It was a very special moment to win the Super Bowl, especially for the Chief," Russell said. "It was a long time coming for him."

And thus began the Steelers NFL dynasty.

5

ICED AWAY

AFC Championship Game
Three Rivers Stadium
Pittsburgh, Pennsylvania
January 4, 1976

AT 6-FOOT-2 AND 300-PLUS POUNDS, "Big" Bob Phelps came by his nickname honestly, and it certainly was beneficial in his career pursuits as a bouncer, bail bondsman, and bounty hunter.

Phelps also worked in the printing industry for 17 years, but that job never put him in contact with people who wanted to do bodily harm to him. Fortunately, he was able to handle himself pretty well until he was forced to go on disability and retire a few years ago. Phelps had back surgery and tore the anterior cruciate ligament and meniscus in both knees while chasing down a man who attempted to jump bail.

"This guy was going away for a long time, and he didn't want to go," Phelps said with a Southern twang in his voice. "So, he ran on me. It was a real rural area, very mountainous, and I blew out both knees while chasing him down. That was something else."

Phelps described his life back then as "a living," not as glamorous as it has been portrayed on the television show *Dog The Bounty Hunter*, noting that the show tends to exaggerate quite a bit about the lead character and his family's exploits in Hawaii as they track down wanted people. First of all, Upper Eastern Tennessee, the

Blountville area in Sullivan County, is nothing like Hawaii in any way. Secondly, the work isn't nearly as interesting.

Sure, it was exciting at times, as Phelps got into his share of hairy situations when people pulled knives on him and had guns, but at least he has never been shot. That's where being "Big Bob" comes into play.

"I went in on one guy, he was bigger than me, and the guy that owned the bonding company told me I definitely was going to have to fight this guy to bring him in," Phelps said. "So I went to his condo with that in mind."

The man lived there with his girlfriend, and she told Phelps that he wasn't around. But since he had a search warrant, Phelps went upstairs to their bedroom to look for him. It was dark, and the far wall had mirrors on it. He was hiding behind Phelps in the closet—and likely could have gotten the jump on him—but must have been impressed by Big Bob and decided to surrender instead. He didn't want to get put away, but he clearly didn't want to get into a fight, either, and gave up without a hassle.

"That's the way you'd like them all to be," Phelps said. "But sometimes, you have to mix it up. That was especially true when I did some bouncer work while I was in the printing industry. I worked for several years at a little place that's not here anymore. It was called The Hitchin' Post.

"That's where Travis Tritt signed his recording contract. They had a circuit that they worked back in the late '80s, and that place was in the circuit for him. The place also received an award from the Country Music Association as the No. 1 live country music honky tonk in the United States. It was just a little hole in the wall, but it was a cool little place."

Phelps recalled several troublesome incidents when brawn was necessary for survival. On one occasion, Phelps and the other bouncers asked a guy who was acting up to leave the building. He obliged but brought back his two brothers and father a short time later for retribution. The father held a large car jack—the kind that would hook to a rear bumper—and swung it like a club. Though it took some time and damaged furniture, that crew eventually saw the light.

Steelers fan "Big" Bob Phelps gives the club's fan base a little Southern flair.

There was another time when Phelps had a *Crocodile Dundee*-sized knife pulled on him. After a few swings, the guy cut Phelps' shirt, but didn't break any skin, and eventually he was disarmed. On another occasion, Phelps actually was shot at, but didn't know it. A guy pulled a shotgun and blasted the front door to the bar. The pellets went through the door and hit Phelps in the leg, but he didn't realize it until later that night.

"I thought it was somebody throwing ice or something like that or maybe a handful of gravel," Phelps said. "But when we took the garbage out at the end of the night, I noticed the security light from the parking lot shining in and could see some little holes in the door where the pellets went through. That was pretty crazy."

Although Mike Webster's barrel-chested, 6-foot-2, 260-pound frame would've qualified him for many of Phelps' dangerous career paths, that was not the reason he was Big Bob's favorite Steeler of all time. In fact, Webster was Phelps' idol since he was young, just nine years old.

Young Bob, not yet Big Bob, was reading a book on up-and-coming players in the NFL before the 1974 season. Webster was drafted in the fifth round by the Steelers that spring, the least famous among four future Hall of Famers in that draft that included Lynn Swann, Jack Lambert, and John Stallworth, and his story intrigued Phelps. He admired Webster for his strength, toughness, tireless training, and conditioning. Though it's easy to see why a young man would feel this way, it just seems a bit odd.

Nowadays, certainly, youngsters are more apt to idolize the more flashy, outspoken players, as Swann was in that Steelers draft—but not Phelps. He was enthralled by Webster's story, his tenure at Wisconsin, and his potential for a lengthy NFL career, and immediately became a Steelers fan. That was the time do to it, too, because the club's bandwagon was quickly filling. The Steelers were coming off back-to-back winning seasons when they went to the playoffs, but were eventually eliminated before reaching the Super Bowl. That changed in 1974, even though Webster didn't play a starting role just yet. He backed up "The Ranger," veteran Ray Mansfield, as the Steelers rolled to the franchise's first Super Bowl title.

"I guess I kind of fell into it that year, but I didn't watch them because they were winning," Phelps said. "And I've always stuck with them even when they starting losing again. But I got interested in them in the first place because of Mike Webster. He was the main reason I liked the Steelers."

The Steelers' success continued in 1975, and they were spectacular after starting the season at 1-1. The club won 11 straight, finishing with a loss at Los Angeles, after they had already clinched the No. 1 spot in the AFC playoffs, ending the regular season with a 12-2 mark. The Steelers were the top team in the AFC again, and the Dallas Cowboys were among the favorites in the NFC, along with the Minnesota Vikings that the Steelers beat in the Super Bowl the previous year.

"I hated the Cowboys," Phelps said. "It was just grand when the Steelers beat them, and I really hoped the two teams would play in the Super Bowl that year. I thought that would just be the greatest thing."

"Iron" Mike Webster was a stalwart on the Steelers offensive line for 15 seasons.

Phelps grew up with three brothers and three sisters, but no one in his family would join him as a Steelers fan, too. The worst was that his younger sister—by less than two years—Julia, just loved the Cowboys. That rivalry in the Phelps household was as intense as it was on the field. Dallas fans, Phelps believed, were not true fans. They were the bandwagon jumpers, those who believed the Cowboys were America's team.

"The Steelers are the blue-collar team," Phelps said. "I've never been fortunate enough to have been to a game, but I try to follow them faithfully and watch them whenever they're on TV.

"And if they're not, we usually try to get together with other Steelers fans in the area. So I feel that I'm a dedicated fan. The fans that get up and leave when the team's losing, I just can't understand that, because they're still the Steelers, and they're still your team."

Phelps believed that the best Steelers fans—the ones who base their interest not on the club's success rate—are comparable to University of Tennessee fans. If the Steelers are Phelps' passion in the NFL, the UT Volunteers hold his heart at the college level. Phelps believed that each team's most faithful fans are dedicated no matter if their club is winning or losing. That's the level that Phelps has attained. He played left offensive tackle and right defensive tackle as a high school football player, so he maintained that interest in the trench players—the guys who do the dirty work, Phelps said—from his formative years. And he always watches both Steelers lines with a discerning eye for blocking assignments, those missed as well as those completed, to gauge the team's play.

In Phelps' view, Webster was as technically sound as any center he has seen; and when his strength was added to the mix, the result was dominant. Although Webster shared snaps with Mansfield for his first two years in the NFL, he began to play more with each passing game. And by the time the 1975 season reached the homestretch, Webster was ready to take charge. The Steelers defeated the Baltimore Colts, 28-10, in an AFC divisional playoff contest at Three Rivers Stadium to set up a title-game matchup against the Oakland Raiders for a second straight season, where the Steelers stunned the Raiders in Oakland the year before to go to Super Bowl IX. Yet this year's game would be played at an icy Three Rivers Stadium. It would be just the right conditions for the Steelers and Webster, in particular, as he and the other offensive linemen liked to disregard the cold and go sleeveless to show off their bulging biceps.

While this game had everything necessary to become an epic clash—and it eventually was voted the best Steelers game in the history of Three Rivers Stadium—a good deal of drama occurred before the teams even took the field. There were snow flurries, and temperatures hovered in the teens (and actually dropped to about minus-15 degrees with the wind chill), so the Raiders were certainly out of their element even though former Steelers defensive end Dwight White didn't believe the inclement weather bothered them as much as it did the southern teams.

"It was worse on Houston," White said. "The Oilers hated to come to Pittsburgh late in the season. But the Raiders, they were our most intense rivals. We had a real good professional rivalry with them, and they were almost at parity with us. But those games were bloodbaths. Of all the other rivalries, Cleveland and Houston, the one with the Raiders was ratcheted up one notch more."

That the Raiders believed they were cheated with the Immaculate Reception play in 1972 certainly enhanced the rivalry. The Steelers, however, had several complaints about their opposition during the 1973 playoff loss at Oakland as well. But when the Steelers returned there in 1974, they dominated a favored Raiders team, that didn't sit too well with the Silver and Black faithful, either. So, the rivalry was stewing as the teams prepared for the 1975 AFC title game; and it reached a boiling point in the days just before gameday.

Steelers head groundskeeper Steve "Dirt" Dinardo explained the situation. "We were covering the field with a regular canvas tarp," Dinardo recalled. "We put weights around it, and then we blew it up. (Oakland coach) John Madden came in that afternoon, and we were painting underneath that cover, like a makeshift tent. The hot air blows the tent up. He said if we kept the field that way for the game, it would be super."

The field conditions were anything but super after what transpired overnight. It was wicked, Dinardo said, as about 25–mph winds cracked the tarp in half, making it uncontrollable. It was removed but, then moisture got underneath the tarp and froze the Three Rivers Stadium turf in certain spots. The field turned to ice, and since its majority would be in the shadows, melting the ice on the sidelines was a nightmare. Dinardo and his crew used steam machines to melt the ice and then hoped to squeeze it off the field. With conditions remaining horrendous on game day, that plan didn't work too well.

"The story goes that I put a hose on the field the night before to freeze the sidelines to help the Steelers and hurt the Raiders," Dinardo said. "That wasn't true, but Madden was so mad."

Oakland liked to utilize its team speed by going around the ends on rushes and running sideline passes with its slick receiving corps, including the speedy Cliff Branch, but Madden argued that those plays would be ineffective under the icy conditions. And the Steelers could run up the middle and off-tackle all day. It sounded like a built-in excuse for the Raiders, Dinardo noted, but the game would be played nonetheless.

The first three quarters were a brutal, hard-hitting defensive struggle with the only points scored by Steelers place-kicker Roy Gerela on a 36-yard field goal midway through the second quarter. Steelers safety Mike Wagner set it up by intercepting Oakland quarterback Kenny Stabler and returning it 20 yards to near midfield. Steelers quarterback Terry Bradshaw then connected with Lynn Swann for 26 yards to get deep into Raiders territory; and a Franco Harris run got the club into field-goal range for Gerela.

The Raiders defense appeared to set the tone early with two first-quarter interceptions, but the Steelers defense responded with tremendous stands and held them to a missed 38-yard field-goal attempt by George Blanda. Gerela missed on two attempts, from 44 and 48 yards in the third quarter, though, which kept the score close. Turnovers were also a factor. The Steelers lost all five of their fumbles, while Oakland lost three of four. Bradshaw was picked off three times, while Wagner intercepted Stabler twice.

"We were just relentless," Wagner said. "The guys up front, especially Dwight White and Ernie Holmes, outplayed their big linemen—Art Shell and Gene Upshaw. We knew we had to play well, but it was a playoff game; and we just rose to the occasion against them. Still, it was a tough game."

Lambert recovered three fumbles for the Steelers, including two in the fourth quarter that led to touchdowns. After allowing 70 yards rushing in the first half, the Steelers limited the Raiders to just 23 in the second half. Harris and the Steelers' running game didn't fare much better with less than 50 yards through three quarters, but the two exploded in the fourth. After Lambert's second fumble recovery, Harris bolted for a 25-yard scoring run around the left end less than a minute into the quarter on a play that should have been stopped for no gain. A trap up the middle was jammed by the Raiders, so Harris broke it off outside, shaking loose from two attempted tackles.

"I turned the corner, saw John Stallworth throw one helluva block, and that was it," Harris said.

Stallworth actually took out two Raiders, headhunting safety Jack Tatum and middle linebacker Monte Johnson, as Harris raced practically untouched into the end zone for a big touchdown. The

Raiders came right back with a 60-yard scoring drive in six plays and less than two minutes to get within 10-7, as tight end Dave Casper made three spectacular catches of 21, 11, and 12 yards to keep the drive alive. Stabler connected with wideout Mike Siani from 14 yards out for the touchdown.

With Swann out of action due to a concussion suffered in the third quarter when he was clotheslined by Oakland safety George Atkinson, Stallworth looked to make another big play—this time a more conventional one for him—less than three minutes after the Raiders scored. He didn't want to just block for a big play, Stallworth told Bradshaw, he wanted to catch a touchdown pass. And on third down from the Steelers 20, Bradshaw called Stallworth's number.

The play didn't go exactly as designed, but great players make exceptional plays when they need to the most. And this catch by Stallworth was spectacular. Colzie had Stallworth covered nearly the entire time, but Bradshaw threw the ball up for grabs anyway.

"I had to run a different route, because Colzie lined up differently," Stallworth said. "When I got to the end zone, I saw him out of the way and behind me. Then I saw him fall down. I just went up in the air and caught it."

Although Gerela missed the extra point, the Steelers still had a two-score advantage, 16-7; but 9:31 still remained. The teams traded possessions, and the Steelers eventually got the ball back with about two minutes remaining. Bradshaw had to keep the drive alive with a scramble for a first down, but he was drilled on the play and suffered a concussion. Terry Hanratty replaced him, apparently just to hand off to Harris or Rocky Bleier. But two plays later, Harris fumbled away the possession with 1:38 left.

The Raiders drove into Steelers territory, and Madden surprised many by attempting a field goal. Blanda nailed it from 41 yards out, and Oakland trailed 16-10 with 17 seconds remaining. The ensuing onside kick was bobbled by Steelers reserve Reggie Garrett, the team's fifth fumble, and recovered by the Raiders at their 45 with just seven seconds left. There was time for two quick plays, one to the sideline and a final one in the end zone.

"We wanted to let them catch a pass and then tackle them inbounds," Lambert said. "That would run out the clock."

Stabler dropped back to pass and saw Branch open downfield, as Steelers cornerback Mel Blount slipped on the icy turf.

"I told Madden it was the same for everybody, but he didn't believe me," Dinardo said. "Both teams had trouble slipping and holding on to the ball."

Dinardo and his staff actually had the field in good condition, considering the circumstances. Dinardo took care of the Steelers home field during its entire existence at Three Rivers Stadium. He worked for the Pirates at Forbes Field as a part-time night-game guy for 10 years, and then "they asked me to come down to Three Rivers Stadium, since I was in construction my entire life. I walked in there the first day it opened in 1970 and stayed 30 years," Dinardo said.

By his account, Dinardo met "a lot of beautiful people" during that time, including the Rooney family and favorite players like Jack Ham and Joe Greene, among others. Dinardo said he eased Ham into retirement after noting that an injury caused him to lose a step or two.

"I told him he looked like a horse running on a bad ankle, and you know what they do to horses like that," Dinardo laughed. "They put them out to pasture. He was limping so bad he retired the next year."

Dinardo recalled that Steelers offensive guard Gerry "Moon" Mullins was so nervous before games that he had to take medicine to calm his stomach. Dinardo surmised that it was because Mullins played at about 200 pounds soaking wet and had to go up against 300-pound defensive linemen every game. But Mullins was strong and quick and used that to his advantage. That helped against a big Oakland front seven in that AFC title game after the 1975 season, while the Raiders offensive front had a tough time with the Steelers defensive front wall.

Oakland was able to hold out the Steelers defense a few times during the fourth quarter, including the waning seconds, as Stabler fired the pass toward Branch. He hauled it in for just his second catch, but it went for around 30 yards and would have put the

Raiders into position to throw the ball into the end zone. But Blount recovered from his slip in time to tackle Branch inbounds, as the clock ran out.

The game—later dubbed "The Ice Bowl" and voted the greatest Steelers win at Three Rivers Stadium—was over, and it put the franchise in the Super Bowl for a second straight season.

"That game was really something, really an exciting game," Steelers owner Dan Rooney said. Dan's father, Art Rooney Sr., guided the team back then, but the son took over a few years later.

Webster supplanted Mansfield as well and would continue a Hall of Fame career. His life ended tragically on September 24, 2002, and Phelps ironically learned about it on his birthday the next day. Webster was diagnosed with brain damage in 1999 from "taking too many hits to the head," and had a heart attack three years later. He was homeless for a time, living in his car, and just recently had returned to the Steelers family, reconnecting with former teammates and the Rooneys.

"For a guy like that, Iron Mike, to suffer like that in his final years was tragic," Phelps said. "That just broke my heart. I had a No. 52 Mike Webster jersey made for me in honor of him. He was really something. He was a perfect guy to play in Pittsburgh for the Steelers."

And he was one of the reasons the Steelers put the Raiders' Super Bowl dreams on ice for yet another season.

6

BACK HOME AGAIN

Super Bowl X
Orange Bowl
Miami, Florida
January 18, 1976

MOST PITTSBURGH STEELERS FANS BELIEVE that
cheering for their hometown team is their birthright; but for Nick
Nery, it's the truth.

Nery, who grew up in the Baldwin, Scott Township area and
attended Canevin Catholic High School, was born to be a Steelers
fan. His father, Carl Nery, an offensive guard selected in the eighth
round from Duquesne University in 1940, played for the Steelers
from 1940 to 1941.

"I was black and gold brainwashed at a very young age," the
younger Nery said. "My dad's 89 years old, and he's fighting for his
life right now after having open-heart surgery in January. He might
be the oldest living former Steelers player.

"For my dad, Sundays involved two main things. That's going to
church and then watching the Steelers."

Nick has maintained a passion for the Steelers that his father, who
passed away after this interview was completed, instilled at a young
age. While he has moved back and forth to the Pittsburgh area several
times, he is always drawn back to cheer for the Steelers. He now lives
in the city's South Hills suburbs.

Now that he's back in Pittsburgh, Nery has decided to help displaced fans follow their beloved Steelers. He remembers what it was like while he was away from home and has tried to help former Pittsburgh natives create fan clubs to draw those with like interests—primarily the Steelers—together as a social outlet, to support their team and also keep in touch with their old hometown. But it hasn't been easy.

Nery joined a Steelers fan club in 1987 while he was in Atlanta, shortly after a dramatic introduction to its president. While he was driving down a street in Atlanta, a Lincoln Continental that had been following him for some time began blowing its horn. Nery pulled over, and so did the Lincoln. A man in a dark suit got out and walked toward his car. Instead of being concerned or angry that the man appeared to be stalking him, Nery was just curious.

"Hey, yinz from Pittsburgh?" the man asked. It was Nery's first meeting with Al Kleber, transplanted in Atlanta from McKeesport, who first started a Steelers Club in Richmond, Virginia in 1968. He later began one in Atlanta after moving there and noticed that Nery's vehicle had a Pittsburgh car-dealer's frame surrounding his Georgia license plate.

"The minute I heard 'yinz,' I knew where he was from," Nery said. "He said that to everyone because he was proud of being from Pittsburgh. After just a few meetings, I realized that these people had a lot more going for them than just black-and-gold sports. They were good people who had a lot of interesting stories about their time in the Pittsburgh area."

Nery moved back to Pittsburgh in 1989 after a decade in Atlanta, about the time that the Chuck Noll era was winding down, and Bill Cowher was just a few years from taking over for him as the Steelers head coach. Nery followed the transition intently, and he also attempted to keep other Steelers fans informed about the team. He believed that even if people left Pittsburgh, they could keep a piece of the city with them through a Steelers club. But Nery has found his task to be difficult.

It seems that, while the vast majority want to go to area sports bars to watch the Steelers play on a weekly basis during football season, few want to get involved to the extent where they can begin a club or even get involved with an existing club wherever they have moved. In an attempt to facilitate fan involvement, Nery has worked closely with Harvey Aronson—known affectionately as "Mr. Steeler" by his friends—through several websites.

While Nery doesn't mind promoting the Steelers and his hometown, he wishes he could get more help from the team. The Steelers conduct a great deal of projects for the local community, but they don't promote fan clubs. Conversely, the team's arch-rivals, the Cleveland Browns, have a paid team representative to help organize support for their loyal fan base. On the Browns website, there's a listing for "Browns Backers." The worldwide membership is 48,579 fans in 279 different clubs, the largest being the Southwest Browns Backers in Phoenix, Ariz. with 2,037 members.

Surely, the Steelers have more fans around the world, Nery wondered.

"I'm sure there are, but they're just not all organized," Nery said. "There's nothing like getting together to watch a Steelers game, no matter where anybody lives, but it's a lot tougher to see them if you don't live in Pittsburgh. That's why it's worth starting or joining a fan club."

While it's great to watch the Steelers on television, nothing beats seeing a game in person. That's why Nery and some buddies from college decided to take a trip to Miami in January 1976. The Steelers were back in the Super Bowl for a second consecutive year, facing the Dallas Cowboys, and those crazy college students believed a road trip to Super Bowl X was the perfect graduation present to themselves.

"We thought it would be a great game, so we tried to buy some cheap tickets," Nery said. "But we just couldn't find any. We still went to the stadium and saw all these kids climbing up a wall to get in, so we decided to try it. It was about 15-20 minutes before the game.

"I got up the wall, but fell off before I could get over and hurt my back. I later found out that I'd slipped a disc in my back. So, we ended up going back to our hotel room and watching the game from there on TV. I thought we'd have a better time at the game, but at least we gave it a shot."

And at least Nery and his friends saw a great game between the Steelers and Cowboys, future Hall of Fame quarterbacks Terry Bradshaw and Roger Staubach, and two terrific defenses. The Steelers were 12-2 that year, tying Minnesota and Los Angeles for the best records in the NFL even though they lost their last game on the road to the Rams after they had already clinched the top playoff spot.

The Steelers were a power-running offensive team with Franco Harris (1,246 yards and 10 touchdowns) and Rocky Bleier, but second-year wideouts John Stallworth and Lynn Swann had secured starting spots and were beginning to make an impact in the league. Swann led the Steelers with 49 catches and 11 TDs that fall, along with a 15.9-yard average, while Stallworth averaged 21.2 yards on just 20 catches with four scores. Bradshaw completed nearly 58 percent of his passes for 2,055 yards and 18 touchdowns with just nine interceptions.

Defensively, it started up front with the Steel Curtain of Joe Greene and Ernie Holmes at the tackle spots and L.C. Greenwood and Dwight White as ends. Jack Ham, Jack Lambert, and Andy Russell were the linebackers, while the secondary was comprised of Mel Blount and J.T. Thomas as the cornerbacks and Mike Wagner and Glen Edwards as the safeties.

Russell's lengthy Steelers career was winding down, and there was nothing more that he would love than to win another Super Bowl title before he retired; and he believed that the Steelers had an excellent chance to repeat as the NFL champions that season.

"We basically had the same team that we had the year before when we won it, but we were a little more experienced," Russell said. "Our defense was still playing great, and the offense was playing better, too. Bradshaw was more experienced; Franco and Rocky were running well; and Swann and Stallworth were coming into their own. We had a really good team."

The Steelers handled Baltimore in the divisional playoffs, the opening round, and had a second straight matchup with the Oakland Raiders in the AFC championship game. The Steelers whacked the

Raiders in Oakland the year before on their way to their first Super Bowl title in their initial appearance. It also was the fourth straight year that the Steelers and Raiders met in the playoffs. The Steelers won the Immaculate Reception game in 1972, lost in a blowout in Oakland in 1973, and then won at home in 1974.

While the Cleveland Browns were always considered to be the Steelers' biggest rivals, the Oakland Raiders were hated the most by Steelers fans and players alike.

"If you think the Cleveland rivalry was like a skirmish, Oakland was a bloodbath," White said. "It was ratcheted up one notch more. But the Raiders, we had a real good professional rivalry with them. It's just that it was more than between the players on the field. The two coaches, Chuck (Noll) and John Madden, and their owner, Al Davis, all had something to say."

The Raiders were livid after the Steelers beat them 16-10 for the right to go to the Super Bowl that year. Davis and Madden said the Steelers altered the field conditions at Three Rivers Stadium on purpose, freezing the turf to make it difficult for the Raiders offense to get untracked. But both teams had to play on that field, and the Steelers earned the right to face Dallas in Super Bowl X. But they might have to do it without Swann.

Early in the game against the Raiders, Swann was drilled by Oakland's headhunting safeties Jack Tatum and George Atkinson, and he received a concussion. After spending two nights in the hospital, Swann slowly began to work out again to prepare for the Super Bowl. But he was listed as doubtful practically until game time. Reports surfaced that he and Bradshaw had difficulty working out their timing problems in practice, and it was still unknown if Swann would even be medically cleared to play. Once that happened, it was up to Swann to determine if he could play.

Swann made an immediate impact, but the Steelers special teams actually helped account for the first points in the game—just not in a good way. Dallas took an early lead less than five minutes into the game when Steelers punter Bobby Walden fumbled the snap to him, and Cowboys tight end Billy Joe Dupree recovered at the Steelers 29. Staubach immediately went to the air and connected with wideout Drew Pearson down the middle, a 14-yard pass that Pearson took all the way into the end zone. Walden acknowledged that the fumble was his fault and noted that he just took his eyes off the ball, but "that happens sometimes."

The Steelers tied the score a short time later, as Swann hauled in a 32-yard pass from Bradshaw down the right sideline to change field position. Swann beat Dallas cornerback Mark Washington on the play, like he would do all day, and somehow Bradshaw threaded the pass along the sideline. The strong-armed quarterback later connected with seldom-used tight end Randy Grossman for the touchdown from seven yards out. Grossman had just 11 catches for the Steelers that season and one touchdown, and the sure-handed receiver had just five career touchdowns with the Steelers. But none were bigger than this one in the Super Bowl.

In eight plays, the Steelers had moved 67 yards under the steady hand of Bradshaw, who had completed the only two passes he attempted.

The scoring play was somewhat of a novelty for Noll. In his coaching career, when the Steelers were deep in an opponent's territory, Noll usually used a power-running offensive set with guard Gerry "Moon" Mullins lining up as an eligible pass catcher but actually as a third tight end.

"Early in the game, we ran out of that formation to give them a look at it," Grossman said. "Then, we threw the pass, and I was wide open."

Dallas place-kicker Toni Fritsch kicked a 36-yard field goal to give the Cowboys the lead again 10-7 early in the second quarter, but the Steelers came right back as Bradshaw hooked up with Swann for 53 yards on a third-and-6 play from the 10 that helped set up a 36-yard field goal attempt right before the half ended. Washington went down on the play and Swann tripped over him, but he still made the juggling catch to set up Gerela. However, the veteran place-kicker failed to convert, as his 36-yard field goal attempt sailed wide to the left. So, the Cowboys led 10-7 at halftime.

Thomas intercepted Staubach early in the second half and returned it 35 yards to set up another Gerela field goal, but he missed

MICHAEL ZAGARIS/GETTY IMAGES

Steelers wideout Lynn Swann's career was filled with acrobatic catches, but his performance in Super Bowl X was even more stunning than usual.

again from only 33 yards out; and the third quarter remained scoreless. However, the Steelers finally got a break about four minutes into the fourth quarter. Reserve running back Reggie Harrison blasted free up the middle and blocked Dallas punter Mitch Hoopes' kick. The ball rolled out of the end zone for a Steelers safety, their second in two Super Bowls, to cut the lead to 10-9.

Ironically, this was Harrison's first blocked punt in his career. That includes his high school days, at Northeast Oklahoma Junior College, and the University of Cincinnati. So, this accomplishment was astonishing to all parties involved, from Dallas coach Tom Landry—who lamented that the Cowboys barely brush-blocked Harrison—to Harrison, who was simply amazed.

"I was yelling and screaming so much that when I went to the bench I didn't realize that we got some points," Harrison said, his mouth bleeding profusely after getting nailed there with the ball. "We were losing, and ... the next thing I remember is that we were lining up to kick off. I looked up at the scoreboard, and we were winning 12-10. I had to ask (Steelers cornerback) Jimmy Allen what happened."

After the free kick, the Steelers drove to the Dallas 20, and Gerela finally made a field goal from there. This time, his 36-yard kick gave the Steelers a 12-10 advantage. Steelers safety Mike Wagner picked off Staubach, the second interception that the future Hall-of-Fame quarterback threw, and returned it to the 7. But the Steelers couldn't punch it in, so Gerela had to kick an 18-yard field goal to give them a 15-10 lead. Still, Staubach and the Cowboys had more than six minutes to regain the lead.

The Steelers defense, led by its formidable front line, held Staubach in check. They harassed him incessantly throughout the game and recorded a Super Bowl-record seven sacks overall. Their consistent pressure also allowed for the Steelers linebacking corps to drop into pass coverage, making it tough for Staubach to find an open receiver. He couldn't do anything on that ensuing possession, and Hoopes was forced to punt.

Edwards, in his role as a punt-returner, ran back the deep kick to the 30. But two smashes into the line netted just six yards for the Steelers, and Bradshaw was forced to drop back to pass on third-and-4 with less than four minutes remaining in the game. Dallas linebacker D.D. Lewis and safety Cliff Harris blitzed on the play, and Lewis got to Bradshaw first, but the quarterback ducked under the hit attempt to gain more time. Bradshaw then uncorked a long pass downfield just before Harris nailed him from the blind side. Harris had several run-ins with the Steelers in his career, but he always seemed to talk a better game than he ever played against them. And his jaws were flapping in overdrive before Super Bowl X.

Harris basically warned Swann that running a crossing route could be dangerous—not that he would try to hurt him, but another big hit could inflict permanent damage on the Steelers wideout. He also patted Gerela on his helmet after a missed field goal in the game, and, disgusted, Jack Lambert slammed Harris to the ground shortly thereafter in a move that would rally the Steelers. Swann shrugged off Harris' veiled threat and played the game of his life. He already had three catches for 97 yards, including two that were highlight-reel specials. This Super Bowl, as much as any game in Swann's career, molded his reputation as the game's most acrobatic receiver. But he also proved to be quite tough, despite a slight build.

"We really didn't know what would happen to Swanny," Bleier said. "He wasn't doing too well leading up to the game, and we didn't know how things would work out. He just didn't look good, but after the opening kickoff he was ready to go—and he was on top of his game from the outset. That's for sure. It really was something special to see."

Swann's performance to that point was amazing, not only considering that he had not practiced much the previous week due to the concussion and two-night hospital stay, but also because the Cowboys were clearly gunning for him throughout the game. That didn't stop Swann from torturing the Cowboys and Washington from the opening kickoff, and he breezed past the Dallas cornerback on one final post route as the all-out blitz left him in unenviable single-coverage once again. Washington leaped in an attempt to knock the ball away, but Swann hauled in the perfect spiral near the goal line and cruised in for the 64-yard touchdown catch.

The pass from Bradshaw was spectacular, not just because it traveled some 70 yards in the air, but since the Steelers quarterback never saw its completion. He was drilled by Harris shortly after releasing the ball and laid unconscious on the ground while the play developed. Gerela missed the extra point, but the Steelers held a 21-10 lead with 3:02 remaining.

Fighting the clock was nothing unusual for Staubach, and in less than a minute, the Cowboys were on the scoreboard again. Starting on his 20-yard line, Staubach passed to Charley Young for seven yards, to Drew Pearson for 30, and to former Steelers player Preston Pearson for 11. The Steelers had a short sack, but Staubach hooked up with a leaping wideout Percy Howard in the end zone from 34 yards out. Fritsch converted to cut the Steelers advantage to 21-17 with time running out.

A Dallas onside kick failed, and the Steelers began their next series at the Cowboys 42 with 1:47 remaining. Terry Hanratty replaced Bradshaw, on the bench and still woozy from Harris' big hit, and he was ordered to run the football. Franco Harris lost two yards on first down but regained it on second. Bleier slammed the line on third down, but gained just one yard. The Cowboys called a timeout after each run, so 1:28 remained with the Steelers in a fourth-and-9 situation at the Dallas 41. Certainly, the Steelers would punt to pin the Cowboys deep in their own territory, yet Bleier slammed the line again on fourth down and picked up just two yards. So, the Cowboys took over on their 39 with 1:22 remaining. The clock stopped on the possession change.

Staubach ran for 11 yards on first down and hooked up with Preston Pearson for 12 to cross midfield. But time remained only for deep routes. Staubach misfired to Drew Pearson on first down, and the second to Howard fell incomplete as well. Staubach's third-down pass intended for Drew Pearson in the end zone was intercepted by Edwards and returned to the 30 to run out the clock and give the Steelers a second straight Super Bowl title.

Despite his team's success, Noll did not get too many accolades along the way, and he was questioned at least twice in Super Bowl X. The first came on the long bomb to Swann. Noll believed that the Cowboys were susceptible to a long pass, even though the Steelers had ran the ball well against them, and he also was chided for running on four straight downs at the end of the game when a punt would have appeared to be more prudent.

"That left them with no timeouts, and they needed a touchdown to win," Noll explained. "If they needed a field goal, it would have been different. I like my defense in that situation. We already had a problem with our punt, so I preferred my defense's chances there as opposed to a punt."

The Steelers became the third NFL team to win consecutive Super Bowls. They matched the 1972-73 Miami Dolphins and 1967-68 Green Bay Packers. Swann won the MVP award with four catches for 161 yards and that amazing 64-yard touchdown reception, something Nick Nery will never forget.

"That was a great catch," Nery said. "I don't remember a lot from that game, since I was in a lot of pain from my pregame fall, but you always see that one in highlights on NFL Films."

And it keyed the Steelers' return home to the Super Bowl.

7

BEHIND ENEMY LINES

Three Rivers Stadium
Pittsburgh, Pennsylvania
September 24, 1978

TOMMY BARNES WANTS to make things perfectly clear: He's a Pittsburgh Steelers fan through and through, always has been and always will be. Even though he's been a Cleveland police officer the past decade, there's surely something black and gold underneath that uniform.

But Barnes wants to clarify something else, too. He has become a Cleveland Browns fan as well. Before his friends and family take issue with that statement, along with his classmates from Beaver High School in Beaver County—about 30 miles north of Pittsburgh— know that Barnes never roots against the Steelers and certainly not when they play the archrival Browns.

However, Barnes didn't go to the dark side so easily. He was heavily wooed by the Browns' organization. Shortly after moving to Cleveland in 1996, following a year as an Atlanta police officer and a stint at the Olympics, Barnes was approached to do extra work as game security for the Browns. His initial job was to escort the referees back and forth from the locker room to the field and to their vehicles after the game. During the game, he also provided field security.

"My wife, Kristin, missed her family too much, so I took the test to be a Cleveland police officer," Barnes said. "That was as close to home as we could get, and it's worked out great. The Browns have treated me so well. They've taken very good care of me and my family, but they're like that with everybody in their organization. They really are a great group of people."

On one occasion, Barnes' loyalties appeared to be tested, like when he had to return to the Steelers locker room with the officials. They asked Steelers head coach Bill Cowher several odd questions, Barnes said, like whether or not his quarterback was right-handed or left-handed and if they could expect any trick plays. Cowher sized up Barnes in his Cleveland police uniform and immediately believed he was a spy, Barnes thought, so the Steelers coach wasn't too free with information while Barnes was in the room.

After escorting the officials for a while, Barnes replaced his police officer's uniform with a suit and tie and moved upstairs at the stadium. Barnes worked in the private boxes and suites and eventually moved to the owner's box where he was approached by Browns security chief Lewis Merletti, once the head of the U.S. Secret Service under President Bill Clinton, and asked if he wanted to be the driver and security for then Browns president Carmen Policy and his family. Policy, the former San Francisco 49ers president, came to the Browns in 1999 then stepped down in 2004.

Barnes, now a detective in the Fourth District Vice Unit for the city of Cleveland, accepted and occasionally drove Policy and his family back to their hometown of Youngstown, Ohio, and to any special event or engagement in the Cleveland area. During that time, Barnes and his family—wife Kristin and children Bobby, 13, Britain, 12, and Brooklyn, 11—became friends with the Policy family, and Tommy enjoyed working for them.

"It was a great job," Barnes said. "He knew I was a Steelers fan because I grew up in Pittsburgh, and he made it a point to get me four tickets for each Steelers game in Cleveland and in Pittsburgh. When Browns owner Al Lerner died, Randy, the son, took over and got rid of everybody, but Carmen and his family were great people.

"They treated us very well. I don't hate the Browns. They help put food on my table, so I cheer for the Steelers all the time. But

Tommy and Kristin Barnes proudly display the Steelers colors, even though they live in Cleveland.

when the Browns aren't playing them, I cheer for the Browns. That's just how it is."

Kim and Chris Villella don't let their brother-in-law's allegiance to the Browns affect their family's relationship with him. Kim and Kristin are sisters, and they are close; so Tommy's not banned from the Villella home by any means. In fact, the Villellas are all too glad to invite the Barnes family to family functions, at least for entertainment purposes.

"Yeah, we like to give him a hard time about that," Chris said. "But that's all right, because Tommy's a good guy. And it doesn't matter who else he cheers for—even if it's the Browns—as long as he cheers for the Steelers, too. And we all know that he's a Steelers fan deep down in his heart. He's not really a Browns fan. He just happens to work for them."

Barnes' fellow Cleveland policemen still like to give him some good-natured ribbing about the Steelers as well, but they haven't been able to say much lately, Barnes noted, because the Browns haven't held up their end in the rivalry. The storied series began in 1950, and it was tied at 55-55 through the 2006 season. The Steelers swept both games then, have won seven straight and are 20-3 since winning the second game in the home-and-home series at Three Rivers Stadium in 1993. The Browns left for Baltimore, and there was no NFL franchise in Cleveland from 1996-98.

Those were the Barnes family's first three years in Cleveland, and Tommy said it was a difficult time for the Browns' legion of fans. He noted that some Cleveland fans became Steelers fans during that time, but they probably wouldn't admit it, and quickly went back to being obnoxious Browns fans when the franchise returned for the 1999 season. The experience wasn't too bad for Barnes, though, because the Steelers were televised as the local game every week, and Steelers news was more readily available. Now, it's back to being all Cleveland Browns football all the time in the area.

"With the internet, I can get Steelers information anytime I want, but you wouldn't believe how it is here," Barnes said. "Cleveland is exactly like Pittsburgh when it comes to football. The only difference is the Super Bowl championships that Pittsburgh has won. Cleveland can't come close to that, of course, but it's unbelievable how loyal the fans are to this city and their team even though the Browns really stink right now."

Barnes still works at Browns home games for new owner Randy Lerner and usually escorts his children around the area. He doesn't get to enjoy the games too much, though, because he's working and really isn't a spectator. He did have a chance to see the Steelers beat the Miami Dolphins in the NFL opener at Heinz Field September 7, 2006, because it was the only game on the schedule. Mostly, though, he's stuck watching Browns games each week.

"There's a few Steelers fans in the area, and a couple guys I work with are from Pittsburgh," Barnes said. "They're big Steelers fans, but I can't find too many out there. And the last few years, Browns fans have had to leave us alone, because the Steelers beat them all the time or they usually find some way to lose. But they just can't beat the Steelers anymore."

Cleveland appeared to be on its way to beating the Steelers during the fourth game in the 1978 season at Three Rivers Stadium, even though the Steelers held the upper hand for much of that era.

Though the early game had no real bearing on the season at large, both teams were 3-0 and the rivalry was as strong as ever.

The Steelers defense, which had a string of 10 quarters without allowing a touchdown, set the tone early by intercepting Cleveland quarterback Brian Sipe on the game's first play from scrimmage. This led a field-goal drive by Steelers place-kicker Roy Gerela. The Browns responded with two field goals by their kicker, Don Cockroft, who added another one in the third quarter to give the Browns a 9-3 advantage going into the fourth quarter.

But the Steelers offense steadily picked up some speed in the second half, and their defense tightened considerably. The Steelers offense rolled to 260 total yards, while the Browns were limited to just 54. Gerela would cap two consecutive fourth-quarter drives with field goals to tie the score at 9-9 with 2:35 remaining in the game, which eventually went into overtime. That's just what the Steelers wanted. They won the coin toss and took the opening kickoff, but Larry Anderson appeared to fumble. The call was controversial—the officials ruled that there was no turnover—and the Steelers retained possession. Steelers quarterback Terry Bradshaw drove the offense to the 37-yard line and once again into Gerela's field-goal range.

With less than four minutes gone in the overtime period, it was second-and-9, and Bradshaw handed off to running back Rocky Bleier, who proceeded to run off tackle like he did so many times before. Bleier and Franco Harris pounded the opposition incessantly during the Steelers' Super Bowl runs following the 1974 and 1975 seasons, but Bleier's best season was 1976, when he ran for 1,036 yards and scored five touchdowns. He also caught 24 passes for another 294 yards.

"That was a great season for both me and Franco," Bleier said. "We had a dominant defense that season and a powerful offensive line. They made it easy for us. But, mostly, we were successful on offense because we ran the ball a lot that season. And we made some big plays in the passing game."

Bleier and Harris both surpassed the 1,000-yard plateau in 1976, the second pair of running backs to do so since Miami's Larry Csonka and Mercury Morris achieved the feat in 1972. While this was amazing in its own right, it was even more surprising for Bleier after everything he went through. Bleier wasn't the biggest or fastest running back in the NFL, but he had to be among the toughest. After playing collegiately at Notre Dame, the Steelers picked him in the 16th round during the 1968 NFL Draft. But before Bleier could compete for a spot on the team, he was drafted again. This time it was for combat duty in Vietnam. The challenge was daunting for everyone involved in that war, but Bleier faced an even bigger task a few months later.

Bleier was crippled by enemy rifle fire and grenade wounds in both legs, for which he earned both a bronze star and purple heart. But he could barely walk, let alone run, and his dream to play in the NFL appeared to be farther away than ever. It took almost two years for him to overcome the injuries and get into shape to make the Steelers' active roster. Bleier was on injured reserve in 1970, and he made the taxi squad in 1971. He finally made the team in 1972 and earned a starting backfield spot in 1974.

Steelers outside linebacker Andy Russell, a 10-year team captain, was drafted by the Steelers in 1963. Russell, Bleier, center Ray Mansfield, offensive guard Sam Davis, and punter Bobby Walden are the only Steelers from those early years to make it to the Super Bowl in 1974.

"Rocky, he was just an inspirational guy," Russell said. "He came back with some severe injuries, basically a shadow of his former self, but he deserves a lot of credit. He really worked his butt off and gained a lot of weight, and he actually became the fastest Steelers player. He ran a 40 in 4.5 seconds, and nobody else on the team could do that.

"He did it through weight-training. I sometimes make the joke that Rocky is the only NFL running back to run for more than 1,000 yards in the league without changing direction. He always ran straight ahead. But he was a great player for us and a real inspiration to everyone."

Steelers commentator Myron Cope was somewhat of an underdog himself, and he came on board with the Steelers around the same time as Bleier. Cope already was an accomplished writer for

Sports Illustrated, but few believed he could be a successful broadcaster due to his unique voice. Yet Cope lasted 35 years with the Steelers and was cherished by the club's fans. Bleier didn't last as long, of course, but he was just as well loved by the Steelers Nation, as well as his teammates.

"He probably was among the fans' most favorite players," Cope said. "He was a solid back and a good person, but few believed he could make the team. He worked hard and overcame all the odds. It was an amazing story."

Bleier's life story came to life for the public in a book and made-for-TV movie called *Fighting Back*. But none of it would have been possible if he didn't crack the Steelers lineup. And even that didn't come easily.

Harris was injured early in 1974, and so was John "Frenchy" Fuqua. So, Preston Pearson and Bleier were inserted in the backfield. The Steelers were 1-1-1 to open the season, and Bleier said the two played the next game at Houston and started the following one at Kansas City. The Steelers won both to begin a 7-1 streak that keyed the first Super Bowl run. Bleier played a crucial role in that one and the next season's as well, and he hoped to be a big part of another Super Bowl team in 1978.

"He was one of my favorite players," Barnes said. "He was just so tough, and he came so far after Vietnam. Yeah, Jack Lambert and Rocky Bleier would have to be my two favorite Steelers from the 1970s. I remember the early years a little bit, but mostly the later '70s.

"We used to sing the Steelers polka in school and decorate our classrooms in black and gold during the season. And we always watched every Steelers game. Bleier didn't make the Hall of Fame like a lot of the other players, but he was just as important to the team's success."

Steelers safety Mike Wagner believed there were many reasons for the team's success, including a lot of intangibles to go with raw, physical ability, coaching, and hard work. The club built a solid core of players, primarily through the annual draft, early in Hall of Fame coach Chuck Noll's tenure and steadily added talented players every year with the penultimate draft in 1974 bringing future Hall of Famers Lynn Swann at wideout in the first round, Lambert at middle linebacker in the second round, wideout John Stallworth in the fourth round and center Mike Webster in the fifth round.

"We had the type of players, especially on defense, who believed that we would own the fourth quarter," Wagner said. "And that would be enough to push us to a win in any game. I know that Noll and some of the coaching staff used to go crazy during the 1970s about this. During one of Noll's locker-room speeches at halftime, he asked us if we believed we could turn it on and off anytime that we wanted because he was unhappy with our first-half efforts. But there were some players on the team, not including myself, who basically had a couple different gears and switches that could make them play at a higher level."

Bradshaw was one of those players. So, instead of hammering the line against the Browns in that initial meeting in 1978, Bleier quickly handed off to Swann for an apparent reverse. But Swann didn't run the ball, either—he tossed it back to Bradshaw, and the strong-armed quarterback fired it downfield to tight end Bennie Cunningham, the Steelers' No. 1 pick in 1976. Cunningham caught the ball at the 3 and rumbled into the end zone at 3:43 into overtime for the game-winning score. The 37-yard, arching flea-flicker pass resulted in Bradshaw's 100th NFL touchdown connection. Cunningham would catch just 16 passes that season for only two touchdowns, but none were more important.

"That was a huge play," Wagner said. "But I've always had the mind-set that big plays, crucial plays, happen all the time during a game. Some are bigger than others, of course, but it all depends on the situation. Take the Immaculate Reception, for example: If Franco didn't catch that pass and Oakland would have won, quarterback Kenny Stabler's touchdown run to give the Raiders a 7-6 lead would have been the big play, the winning play."

Wagner believed that if the flea-flicker pass from Bradshaw did not occur, another play would have been a key to that win against the Browns like a big run by Harris that helped the Steelers drive inside the Cleveland 40. Gerela could have kicked a field goal from

GEORGE GOJKOVICH/GETTY IMAGES

Safety Mike Wagner roamed the secondary in all four of the Steelers' Super Bowl wins in the 1970s.

there, and he would have been the hero for making four field goals in the game, including the winning boot.

"That game definitely was a defining moment for the Steelers at that time in that rivalry," veteran Steelers beat writer Norm Vargo said. Vargo, who retired as the sports editor for the *McKeesport* (Pennsylvania) *Daily News* shortly after the team moved to Heinz Field, said the Steelers proved they would do whatever it took to win games and return to the Super Bowl.

Since it's been some 25 years since he last suited up for the Steelers, White was a little hazy on the particulars from most games.

"I can remember only about 30 percent of what happened accurately," White joked. "When I think about Cleveland, I remember Cockroft kicking last-second field goals a couple of times to beat us over there. (But) in Pittsburgh, they had a real tough time beating us.

"We ended up dominating the series against Cleveland back then, for the most part, and when you consider interconference rivalries . . . the big number is in Super Bowls. And they just don't have a seat in first class. You know, you ain't done a thing if you ain't got the ring."

The stunning overtime win improved the Steelers record to 4-0 and gave them sole possession of first place in the AFC Central Division race. And it continued the Browns' frustration at their personal house of horrors, making this their ninth straight loss at Three Rivers Stadium.

"They didn't beat us too often back then, and they rarely beat us at Three Rivers," Bleier said. "But we had a really good football team that year, for a number of reasons. . . . We had leadership at the top, the Rooneys and head coach Chuck Noll, and we had some very talented players.

"We came out of that era with nine Hall of Famers. It takes time to build a team like we had in 1978, but it started for us when Chuck got there in 1969. We picked up a few key guys here and there and had the big draft in 1974. We were really good."

The Steelers won three more games in a row to open the 1978 season at 7-0. They lost a home game to the Houston Oilers in Game 8 and a few weeks later at Los Angeles against the Rams, but finished with five straight wins to go 14-2. The Steelers clubbed the Denver Broncos in the divisional playoff round and the Oilers in the AFC title game before beating the Dallas Cowboys to capture the Super Bowl. The Steelers won the NFL title the following year as well to make it four Super Bowl wins in six seasons, which is an unprecedented run of success in the NFL that stands to this day.

Yet, just as Barnes' current run behind enemy lines in Cleveland, the Steelers' success wouldn't have been possible without the Browns.

8

THE BEST
OF THE BEST

AFC Championship Game
Three Rivers Stadium
Pittsburgh, Pennsylvania
January 7, 1979

AARON AND JESSICA NELSON didn't find it under their tree, but the couple's best Christmas present came when they learned that their first child was due around the holidays. Even though nothing compared to that gift, meeting Pittsburgh Steelers quarterback Ben Roethlisberger was thrilling in its own right. Nelson is the head athletic trainer for the NBA's Phoenix Suns, and he's a huge Steelers fan, even though he really has no ties to Pittsburgh. He grew up in Iowa and was a Hawkeyes fan, and their team colors are black and gold. The school officially adopted them after the Steelers' Super Bowl runs in the 1970s to improve their stature, and Nelson became a fan of both football programs.

"Back then, the best two teams in the NFL were probably the Cowboys and the Steelers, and I didn't want to be a Cowboys fan," Nelson said. "Most of my friends were Cowboys fans. Some liked St. Louis and the Bears, but I liked the Steelers. The Cowboys were America's team. Green Bay, Minnesota, and Chicago are nearby, but not really that close to be our team where I lived in Southwest Iowa."

Football is king in Manning, Iowa, Nelson's hometown of approximately 1,200 people, and he couldn't get enough information on the Steelers while growing up. Even though the club went through a rough patch in the 1980s, including a low mark of 5-11 in 1988 that was the team's worst in some two decades, Nelson's faith in his favorite NFL team never waned.

In fact, he recalled one wonderful Christmas around the fourth or fifth grade when he received a Steelers parka for a present. It became his most cherished Christmas present for years—until that recent visit from the stork, of course.

"You can imagine how cold it was in Iowa at that time, 20-30 below (zero) with the wind chill," Nelson said. "So, I loved that parka, and I've been a big Steelers fan ever since."

Nelson, 37, noted that, while he didn't get to see too many Steelers games when he was young, because "there were only 4-5 (TV) stations back then," but all the big games were televised with the Super Bowls at the forefront. Even though he was just five and six years old when the Steelers made their initial two championship runs, the next two from 1978 and 1979 are vivid in his mind, and what he can't remember has been supplemented by videos and highlight shows. But those aren't Nelson's only Steelers memories. He was a football, baseball, basketball, and track star in high school and wore Lynn Swann's No. 88 proudly in his role as a scholastic wideout. Nelson attended Iowa State and quickly became a Cyclones fan, but his faith in the Steelers never waned from those Super Bowl years through the lean times and back to prominence during coach Bill Cowher's 15-year tenure.

"Lynn Swann was my favorite," Nelson said. "I always liked Terry Bradshaw, too, and Franco Harris—his jersey was the first authentic jersey I ever bought. I have six now: Franco, Jerome Bettis, Joey Porter, Troy Polamalu, and Ben Roethlisberger's home and away jerseys. I need to get a Swann jersey. I guess his will be next."

Nelson also used his connections with Reebok, the Suns apparel maker that also works with the NFL, to put together a custom-made No. 7 Roethlisberger jersey for then girlfriend Jessica Dentmeyer. Since she was petite in size, she needed a special jersey made for a special occasion. Nelson wanted to propose to Dentmeyer and concocted a plan for the moment during a fantasy football draft of

Aaron and Jessica Nelson are a pair of fanatic Steelers fans living in Phoenix.

all things, and was wearing his Big Ben jersey at the time. With his first pick in the draft, Nelson selected his girlfriend and asked her to marry him. They both wore Roethlisberger jerseys in their engagement photo. Their family members and friends in attendance were all wearing Steelers jerseys as well.

Having so many Roethlisberger jerseys was beneficial in February 2006, because the Steelers quarterback was expected to be in the Phoenix area for Muhammad Ali's annual Fight Night festivities. Suns superstar Steve Nash, the two-time NBA MVP, also planned to be there with celebrities from around the world. Nash told Nelson that he would get Roethlisberger to autograph a jersey for him, and that thrilled him to no end.

"It was believable to me," Nelson said. "Here's Steve Nash, a star athlete in his own right, carrying around this jersey the entire night until he met up with Roethlisberger. Now, that's a good friend."

Roethlisberger signed it to "Aaron, Congratulations on the engagement. We won it for you." The event occurred right after the Steelers won Super Bowl XL in Detroit. Nash also gave Roethlisberger one of his autographed Suns jerseys, and the two quickly became friends. Roethlisberger visited the Phoenix area again around the Bowl Championship Series (BCS) title game between Ohio State and Florida in January, 2007, and he asked Nash to go to the game with him. Nash couldn't make it, but he asked Roethlisberger to forego golfing with his buddies and come to a Suns practice instead. Roethlisberger quickly agreed.

Nash had to square the deal with Phoenix head coach Mike D'Antoni, who also assumed the added roles of executive vice president of basketball operations and general manager for the Suns in March, 2006, before he could bring Roethlisberger to the arena. The two arrived at the training room through the weight room, basically the back door, to surprise Nelson.

"I think the rest of the guys were probably just as excited as I was or maybe they were just excited for me, because I talk about the Steelers all the time," Nelson said. "I put stuff up on my windows in the training room, so they kill me about it all the time. But we took some pictures, and I got him to sign a basketball for my wife and me.

"We got him practice gear and shoes and everything, and he went through our full shootaround. He watched film, went through the shooting drills and everything. He was pretty athletic, for a football player trying to play basketball, because we've had some guys here before, and he was nothing like them. He did really well."

Nelson got a chance to watch the Steelers' Monday night game in San Diego in 2005 when Bettis hammered the Chargers for key rushing yards, and place-kicker Jeff Reed nailed a game-winning field goal at the end. Coach D'Antoni postponed a Suns training camp practice for a day so Nelson could attend the game; and the team's owner secured four tickets in a box for Nelson and his family members. He also got to see the Steelers at a 2006 preseason game that opened the Arizona Cardinals new stadium, but he hasn't been to a game in Pittsburgh at Heinz Field. That's tentatively on his busy agenda for the future, but impending fatherhood and the NBA's rigorous travel schedule keep him occupied from the fall through the spring.

"It's really tough, but maybe some day I'll get there," Nelson said.

Jessica Nelson's grandparents live in Hershey—near Harrisburg—

a hotbed for Steelers fans. Her family is from New Jersey, so they help extend the Steelers fan base as well; and with Nelson leading the way in Phoenix, the Steelers Nation has moved toward the West, too. Coach D'Antoni is a Cleveland Browns fan, the poor guy, but Nelson got him to wear a Steelers cap during a practice and post-practice interview after a whipping his team took from the Steelers.

The Steelers franchise is among the NFL's best, and the 1978 version is believed to be the best team in NFL history. It ripped through its opposition during the regular season with a 14-2 record, the NFL's initial foray into a 16-game regular season, losing just to Houston at home (24-17) and at Los Angeles to the Rams (10-7) before blowing through the AFC divisional playoff game against Denver (33-10) at home to set up a third matchup with the Oilers.

Under head coach Bum Phillips, Houston had become the Steelers' biggest AFC Central Division rival at the time, but it always had to get past the "Steel Door," as Phillips liked to call it. At one point, he had noted, the Oilers were going to have to "kick that steel door in."

Houston got its first chance in a championship setting in the AFC title game after the 1978 season. The Oilers already won once that season at Three Rivers Stadium, but they also lost at their home, the Astrodome, 13-3, a month earlier. Since the Steelers won the AFC Central crown, Houston was the AFC wild-card playoff team and had to go on the road. The Oilers won at Miami in the wild-card matchup, 17-9, and beat the New England Patriots, 31-14, in Foxboro, Massachusetts, to get a shot at the Steelers.

Quarterback Dan Pastorini and running back Earl Campbell led the Oilers offense, along with tight end Mike Barber and wideouts Ken Burrough, Billy "White Shoes" Johnson, and Mike Renfro. A future Hall of Famer, Campbell ran for 1,450 yards and 13 touchdowns, while Burrough had 47 catches and two scores.

The Steelers had recovered from a sour 1977 campaign when they finished 9-5 and lost for the second time at Denver that season in their AFC divisional playoff matchup, 34-21, at Mile High Stadium. But the Steelers came back to dominate their regular-season schedule in 1978. Running back Franco Harris ran for nearly

1,100 yards and eight touchdowns, but quarterback Terry Bradshaw also had a spectacular season. He completed more than 56 percent of his passes for nearly 3,000 yards and 28 touchdowns. Wideouts Lynn Swann (61 catches and 11 scores) and John Stallworth (41 and nine) combined for more than 100 receptions and 20 touchdowns.

A cold, steady rain that began before the opening kickoff appeared to negate each team's offensive options, but the Steelers got off to a quick start with touchdown runs by Harris from seven yards out and Rocky Bleier from 17 to give their team a 14-3 first-quarter advantage. Then, the Steelers appeared to put the game away with a 17-point outburst just before halftime. Each score was set up by a Houston fumble, which was part of an NFL playoff-record 12 fumbles in the game. Each team fumbled six times. The Oilers lost four, and the Steelers lost three. Swann and Stallworth each caught a touchdown pass from Bradshaw, and place-kicker Roy Gerela added a field goal to give the Steelers a 31-3 halftime lead.

"The first thing I think of with that game is the weather," Steelers outside linebacker Jack Ham recalled. "It was probably the most miserable weather in which I have ever played. Since Houston played in the Astrodome (indoors), it couldn't have been any fun for them, either. Our defense really set the tone early in the game. We forced a lot of turnovers.

"On the first play, Earl Campbell tried running the ball, and L.C. Greenwood made a great play to take on two blockers. That allowed me to stop Earl in the backfield. This game was a classic example of a warm-weather team heading North for the playoffs. That's why you play for home-field advantage during the season."

Bleier said his most vivid memory from that game was Bradshaw sliding on the wet turf at Three Rivers after a long gain. The play is a staple on NFL Films highlight shows from the Steelers in the 1970s, and the play also was immortalized as a cover shot for *Sports Illustrated*.

"We made some big plays early and really took advantage of their turnovers," Bleier said. "Those were the big things in that game."

If there was a turning point in the game, however, it probably occurred during the intermission when the Steelers were able to replace their waterlogged uniforms with dry gear. The Oilers traveled with just one set and had to go back out in rain-soaked uniforms.

"All I remember about that game is that it was cold and wet," Steelers longtime equipment manager Tony Parisi said. "There was a driving rain. It was the coldest game I ever worked in my life. We were able to change our uniforms, and we wore an Acton shoe from Montreal. It was a multicleated shoe with spirals on every cleat, so when you compressed it onto the ground it grabbed. It wasn't a hard material, so you were able to get good traction."

Parisi was a legend among equipment managers in the NFL and dearly beloved by Steelers players since he came to the team in 1965. He was the equipment manager and trainer for the Pittsburgh Hornets hockey club prior to that, but moved to the Steelers because he didn't want to travel so much. Parisi was with the Steelers when they played at Pitt Stadium, Forbes Field, and into Three Rivers Stadium. He retired when "they blew up Three Rivers," Parisi said, and before the club moved to Heinz Field and into the UPMC Sports Complex training facility on Pittsburgh's South Side.

"You can't stand in front of improvement and progress," Parisi said. "That practice facility, it's amazing. They have an equipment manager, an assistant and interns. And the training room is so high class. It's such a big business now with a lot of advances, but that's great."

Parisi was born in Niagara Falls and is a Canadian citizen. In fact, he's the only Canadian with four Super Bowl rings. While he loved football, hockey was his passion. He played minor league hockey and was a goaltender. He played up to the Junior A-League level. After that experience, though, Parisi decided to go overseas and play hockey in England, Sweden, Italy, and Czechoslovakia. After that stint, Parisi played in the International Hockey League (IHL), North American (NAHL) and American (AHL) Hockey Leagues. Parisi eventually played and worked for the Pittsburgh Hornets.

The club folded in the mid-1960s after winning the Calder Cup league championship, and after that Parisi was hired by Art Rooney Sr. to work for the Steelers as their equipment manager.

Parisi noted that he still gets phone calls from former Steelers greats like middle linebacker Jack Lambert, Bleier, and offensive guard Gerry "Moon" Mullins, as well as others. Parisi was well known as an innovator for using the Acton shoes and Maxpro helmets, a clear-shell helmet that was adaptable to any size head, large or small, because the inner pads could be removed and replaced and molded to custom-fit any head size. But his most notable accomplishment with the Steelers, in many fans' minds, is that he unofficially "retired" a handful of uniform numbers permanently.

The following jersey numbers have not been reissued since their former owners retired, although the Steelers do not officially have any retired numbers. The group includes Bradshaw's No. 12, Harris' No. 32, center Mike Webster's No. 52, Lambert's No. 58, Ham's No. 59, and "Mean" Joe Greene's No. 75. Each player was elected to the Pro Football Hall of Fame. Former Parisi assistant and current Steelers equipment manager Rogers Freyvogel continued the custom by holding back the No. 36 jersey worn by running back Jerome Bettis when he retired after the 2005 season. Bettis likely will be inducted into the Hall of Fame as well in a few years.

Linebacker Todd Seabaugh actually was issued No. 59 after he was drafted in 1984, two years after Ham retired, but "he was cut, and that was it," Parisi said. "The others, I just protected them. And who's going to fill Joe Greene's jersey? I did it on my own and was never questioned about it."

Freyvogel also noted that sometime in the near future, he might hold out Stallworth's No. 82 and Swann's No. 88. Both are Hall of Famers. No. 82 was proudly worn by Antwaan Randle El (2002-05), before he left for the Washington Redskins via free agency. Other notables included Yancey Thigpen (1992-97) and Bobby Shaw (1999-01). Wideout Eugene Baker wore No. 82 until he was released in 2006; but no one has it yet in 2007, but tight end Jon Dekker was given No. 88 when he signed as a free agent in 2006 and still wears it. Swann's former number was also worn proudly by Andre Hastings (1993-96) and Courtney Hawkins (1997-2000).

The reason Parisi couldn't "retire" the Swann and Stallworth numbers was that wide receivers could only be given numbers in the

80s. He believed that was done for television viewing purposes. Keeping the numbers uniform—divided by position, in other words—made it easier for fans to follow the game. Beginning last season, however, the NFL relaxed that policy and allowed some wideouts to choose numbers in the teens. Santonio Holmes, the Steelers' No. 1 pick in 2006, wears No. 10, for example.

In the 1978 AFC title game, however, Bradshaw connected with his favorite targets—No. 88 Swann and No. 82 Stallworth—with relative ease. He completed 11 of 19 attempts for 200 yards, while Pastorini was hammered all afternoon by the Steelers defense. He was picked off five times and sacked on four occasions. The "Steel Curtain" also contained Campbell, the NFL's leading rusher and former Heisman Trophy winner, to just 26 yards on 15 carries in the first half and 62 yards on 22 runs overall.

"The Steelers had already won two Super Bowls, and their defense was still great," McKeesport Daily News sports editor Norm Vargo said. "There was a lot of emotion and anticipation for them to do it again; so after two years of missing out, the team and its fans were determined in 1978."

The game was long decided by the time Campbell got a little bit untracked, as the Steelers held a huge advantage in total first-half yardage (287 to 54). The club also was the beneficiary of Theo Bell's six punt returns for 91 yards for more than a 15-yard average, and Ham's dominant performance. The All-Pro outside linebacker recorded an interception, two fumble recoveries, and a sack and was in Pastorini's face all day.

"He had a big game, for sure," Steelers defensive end Dwight White said. "But as I recall, everyone on our defense played well. They couldn't do anything against us, and the conditions were just horrendous. It was cold and wet, and I imagine very tough for a team from Texas that plays indoors."

White said he always believed that the Steelers had a distinctive advantage at home when they played against teams like the San Diego Chargers or Houston Oilers, because the winters in the 1970s were "a lot more brutal than they are now." White has lived in the area some 40 years now, too, so he speaks from experience as a player and fan.

Sure, the Steelers got cold, too, White noted, but Campbell just couldn't adjust. While the jackhammer from Texas was pretty tough in the first half, he wasn't quite as hard-nosed a runner in the second half. And the Oilers weren't quite as tough, either, after the intermission. They were especially easy to push around on this day because they came out in soggy uniforms, while the Steelers were dry and refreshed. And even though it was bitterly cold on that occasion, offensive linemen like Webster and left tackle Jon Kolb would come out early for the second half, before the visiting team left the locker room. White recalled that they put on a show with their tight jerseys, sleeves rolled up and muscles bulging.

"Earl, he'd be peaking out at us and trying to decide if he wanted to come back out for the second half," White said. "And we said, 'Sure Earl, come back out, we want to play some more.' So, with the crowd and the weather, I just thought we had a big advantage at home. Not to mention, too, that we thought we were better than (the Oilers) anyway. But it kind of softened them up a little bit for the second half."

The Steelers only outscored Houston 3-2 in the second half of the 1978 AFC title game, a Gerela field goal to an Oilers safety, but the game was among the most lopsided wins in the club's history and certainly was its largest championship win. The victory also put the Steelers in Super Bowl XIII against the Dallas Cowboys and went a long way toward securing the unofficial title as the best team ever.

9

TIME FOR A CHANGE

Super Bowl XIII
Orange Bowl
Miami, Florida
January 21, 1979

SEAN FRANCIS WASN'T BORN UNTIL 1970, so his earliest memories about the Pittsburgh Steelers centered around St. Ursula's grade school in Allison Park in Pittsburgh's North Hills area with he and his classmates dressing up for special black-and-gold days during football season.

Sean really doesn't remember the first two Steelers Super Bowl wins after the 1974 and '75 seasons, but he started following the club more closely during the second run from 1978-79. Those were the days when everyone in the area took the Steelers for granted, that they would win every Super Bowl and the Pirates would win the World Series, Sean noted.

"I really got interested in the early '80s, when I understood football more," Sean said. "But I remember those early teams, and I've seen videos of the early Super Bowls. The Steelers had some great teams back then."

The Francis family also cheered for the Steelers, and like most families in the Pittsburgh area, Sean said, it was "a family thing for us to watch Steelers games."

Sean's fascination with the Steelers continued into the 1980s even though the team's success did not, but he had other interests as well. Sean attended North Allegheny High School, Allegheny Community College, and Robert Morris, but his career path was not yet set. He trained to be a pilot and actually has 50 hours in a Cessna. Sean also developed a landscaping business on the side and "was making pretty good money." Instead of hiring pilots, though, the airlines were laying off workers. When his flight instructor decided to go back to school, Sean needed to refine his career plans.

"I was making real good money in landscaping, so I moved away from home and got an apartment," Sean said. "Things were going really well for me, but something was missing. I just didn't know what."

Sean was raised as a Catholic, and along with watching Steelers games he said they always said the Rosary as a family. Even though it took just 10-15 minutes, it got them praying together. Sean enjoyed that family time. It didn't make him stick it out as an altar boy, but he remained interested in his religion as he got older and even read a few books along with the Bible.

"I never knew so much about my faith," Sean said. "One night, when I kneeled to pray, I felt like God asked me to give him everything instead of just 20 minutes a night and an hour on Sundays."

Sean didn't know what that meant, but he later believed that he was supposed to become a priest. Since he was in his early 20s, making good money in landscaping and enjoying life, he didn't think too much more about it. And Sean really didn't believe his lifestyle would translate too well into the priesthood—but he later found out that a change was necessary and he wasn't really in control of his future.

"At first," Sean said, "I was like, 'Thanks for the offer, but evidently you've forgotten about my past.' Not that it was so bad, but I just didn't think I was priest material. They were so holy and good, and . . . I really didn't think I would make a good priest. I still questioned what I was going to do with my life, but I didn't think the priesthood was for me."

Steelers fan Fr. Sean Francis with pal Garrett.

Sean figured that God eventually would come to his senses and withdraw his offer, but that didn't happen. He continued to go to mass on a daily basis, and a few years after the initial revelation, everything became more clear. Sean would move back home and move his life in a more spiritual direction. He spoke to his parish priest about it and decided to check out St. Paul's Seminary in Greentree. He was 24 years old at the time, and contrary to what he believed, many others there were close to his age.

Those guys were basically in the same situation as Sean. They needed guidance and believed the church would provide it. Sean took a couple classes there and went every Thursday night for evening mass, dinner, and a class. He didn't live there like some other young men that he met, but Sean spent a good deal of time with them.

"I finally entered the seminary there when I was 26, and that was a huge change in my life," Sean said. "The first few days there I could hardly eat I was so uncertain about everything; but every time I was ready to leave, God would do something to keep me there. After a while, I would come to trust Him more, and I handled everything much better."

After several years at St. Paul's and St.Vincent College in Latrobe, where the Steelers hold their annual training camp workouts in the summer, Sean was ordained a Roman Catholic priest in the spring of 2004, and became Fr. Sean Francis. His first parish was Our Lady of Peace in Conway, about 20 miles from where he grew up and some 25 north of Pittsburgh. It was a long road from Sean to Fr. Sean, but the change was quite fulfilling.

Fr. Sean maintained his interest in the Steelers as well and would watch games with his friends at the seminary and thereafter. He also would attend a couple games a year when his dad got tickets through his work for the Pittsburgh Federation of Teachers. He always wanted to have season tickets, but never thought to get on the waiting list while he was in the seminary. He's been on the lengthy list the past few years, however, and hopes to someday get a call from the Steelers.

"I could have had eight years in, though, so that's tough," Fr. Sean said. "And they said there's about a 15-year wait. So, it'll be a while for me, a long wait, but one day I'll be at the top of the list for season tickets."

Fr. Sean doesn't wear his priest's collar at Steelers games, but he doesn't turn into a raving lunatic either. He just has a few beers and cheers for the team like all the other fans.

"You know, when you're there, you always think you can have an impact when the Steelers are on defense," Fr. Sean said. "You have to yell to keep the opposing players from hearing the snap count and things like that. I'm pretty hoarse after I go to a game, because the refs always seem to be against the Steelers. So, we have to let them know they're wrong."

Fr. Sean gets into the Steelers so much that he occasionally incorporates the team in his Sunday sermons. He usually mentions the team at the end of mass with the weekly announcements and before the final blessing. He mostly refers to them only when an important game is coming up that afternoon and for the most part has received positive feedback. He got the biggest response prior to the final regular-season game in 2005, Jerome Bettis' final home game against Detroit, that the Steelers needed to win to make the playoffs.

"We didn't have a pope at that time, so I basically said there was more of a chance for me to be pope than for the Steelers to lose that game," Fr. Sean said. "I got a lot of feedback from that comment."

Fr. Sean made a slight miscalculation, though, because not all of his parishioners were Steelers fans. As hard as that is to believe in Western Pennsylvania, it's quite true. In fact, several families are actually Cleveland Browns followers. Those people likely are the ones with the highest pain tolerance. But that's another story for another time. Fr. Sean's stories, his homilies, usually tie in personal experiences with family members and friends. That's what makes him such a popular priest, especially among younger parishioners; but some older ones would rather he stick to the scripture readings than use sports references.

"Not too many, but there are a few people who don't like it," Fr. Sean said. "I don't do it all the time, so I really don't see anything wrong with it. One non-Steelers fan said his favorite team is whichever one is playing the Steelers that week. To each his own, I guess, but that's OK."

Even though he believed that fans who were so inclined probably prayed for the Steelers to win, at least in the more important games against the tougher teams, Fr. Sean didn't subscribe to that practice. He would rather pray that nobody gets injured, on both teams for that matter, but not for the Steelers to win. However, he cheers extremely hard to that end.

"You can have strong faith and still love sports," Fr. Sean said. "Sports can be a diversion, but it doesn't have to be anything and everything—even with the Steelers. At least, that's how I look at it. It's why I made a change in my life and became a priest, but I'm still a big Steelers fan."

The Steelers had to make some changes, too, even in their heyday. During their first two Super Bowl seasons, the Steelers were primarily a run-oriented team, pounding the opposition with running backs Franco Harris and Rocky Bleier. But during the second two Super Bowl runs, the passing game developed into a high-powered attack with quarterback Terry Bradshaw and talented, young wideouts John Stallworth and Lynn Swann. Instead of running the opposition into the ground, the Steelers evolved into a big-play, fast-striking offense to go with their ferocious defense.

This combination was difficult to beat, and that Steelers' 1978 squad was believed to be among the best ever. This extreme success was especially gratifying after a 34-21 divisional playoff loss the previous year at Denver. The team vowed to get back to the Super Bowl that season after a two-year absence, and had to open with Denver again in the playoffs. The Steelers had scored playoff wins over the Broncos and the Oilers to earn a date with the Dallas Cowboys in the Super Bowl for the second time in four years.

"Many times we were underdogs early in the 1970s, but we just knew that somehow our offense or defense at the end of the game was going to put us in a position to win," Steelers safety Mike Wagner said. "It didn't always happen that way, but most of the time things went our way.

"So, that's the way we looked at it. . . . Against the Cowboys—especially in our Super Bowls against them—they always seemed to be knocking at the door at the end no matter what happened during the game. So, I just think as a player, you have to think that the big play hasn't occurred and the game hasn't been won until there was no way left for the other team to win."

The Steelers had already beaten the Cowboys in Super Bowl X after the 1974 season, and they had a chance to be the first three-time winner with a rematch against them in Super Bowl XIII after the 1978 campaign. Each team featured a strong defense. The Cowboys led the NFL with just 107.6 rushing yards allowed per game, while the Steelers were at 107.8. And even though Dallas started the season slowly, it was on an eight-game winning streak going into the Super Bowl that included a 27-20 opening playoff win against Atlanta and a 28-0 blowout victory against the Los Angeles Rams in the NFC championship game.

Dallas took the opening kickoff and drove into Steelers territory to the 34, and Tony Dorsett ran for 38 yards in the possession. Then

Quarterback Terry Bradshaw became a big-play passer for the Steelers in the late 1970s.

the Cowboys attempted to take advantage with a big play as Staubach handed off to Dorsett, and he tried to slip the ball to wideout Drew Pearson for an apparent double-reverse, but Pearson fumbled. "It was going to be a pass to (tight end) Billy Joe (DuPree)," Pearson later said. "We ran that play a lot in practice and never messed it up. I don't know how we fumbled. I expected the ball a little lower, but I should have held on."

Steelers defensive lineman John Banaszak recovered near midfield, and seven plays later Bradshaw connected with Stallworth for a 28-yard touchdown to give his team a 7-0 lead.

The Cowboys scored late in the first quarter as defensive end Ed "Too Tall" Jones forced a Bradshaw fumble; and Staubach capitalized by hooking up with wideout Tony Hill, and he tiptoed down the sideline for a 39-yard touchdown. It was the only first-quarter touchdown the Steelers allowed all season.

Bradshaw fumbled again a few minutes into the second quarter. Linebacker Thomas "Hollywood" Henderson stripped Bradshaw, and fellow linebacker Mike Hegman scooped up the ball and returned it 37 yards for the go-ahead score.

Henderson came by his nickname honestly. Though he was a good athlete and a quality linebacker, he was a brash loudmouth as well. Henderson said the Rams were inferior and would be shut out by the Cowboys, which they were; but he then made another bold claim before the Super Bowl, predicting another shutout and then made unfriendly comments about several Steelers players. Bradshaw's talent and intelligence were heavily questioned. Henderson proclaimed that Bradshaw couldn't spell the word CAT if you spotted him the letters C and A. The Steelers refused to get into a war of words with Henderson and the Cowboys, but defensive tackle Mean Joe Greene—never one to back down from any situation—had a brief response.

"We don't have to talk about how good we are," Greene said. "We plan to show that on the football field. We don't talk. We just get the job done."

The Steelers did just that and tied the score at 14-14 when Bradshaw hit Stallworth with a 10-yard pass that he turned into a 75-yard touchdown. This was amazing, not just for Stallworth's spectacular catch and run, but because Bradshaw said he wasn't even the primary receiver. The Steelers quarterback was supposed to throw to Swann, but he was covered.

"I was going to Lynn Swann on the post," Bradshaw said, "but ... (the Cowboys) left Stallworth open. I laid the ball out there, and it should have gone for about 15 yards; but Stallworth broke it and went all the way."

Pittsburgh place-kicker Roy Gerela boomed a 51-yard field goal that was a bit short and hit the crossbar. Dallas had great field position and was moving again on its ensuing drive, but Steelers cornerback Mel Blount stepped in front of a Staubach pass and returned it to the Dallas 29. A few plays later, Bradshaw hit Bleier for a seven-yard score to take a 21-14 advantage into the locker room at halftime.

Nothing much happened through the majority of the third quarter with both defenses holding strong, but Dallas drove deep into Steelers territory to the 10 late in the third. Coach Tom Landry called for a power formation with both tight ends, DuPree and future Hall of Famer Jackie Smith, in the lineup. Instead of running the ball, however, Staubach dropped back to pass on third down and tossed the ball to a wide-open Smith in the end zone.

The Cowboys were a much different team than the one that faced the Steelers in Super Bowl X. Not only did they sign Smith, but they took Dorsett—the 1976 Heisman Trophy winner from the University of Pittsburgh—in the first round in the NFL Draft the following year, and he helped them get back to the Super Bowl as a rookie again in '79 against the Steelers.

"There's one thing with the Cowboys to separate them from the Raiders, Browns, Bengals, or Oilers," Wagner said. "We played Oakland and Houston in a number of (AFC) championship games. But with the Cowboys, they already won a championship before, and they were a good team.

"I think we were respectful as players about what they accomplished to that point. We knew that they knew how to win, and Staubach was deadly. He was a great quarterback, and the 1978 team that they had was a great team. And when they picked up Dorsett, they picked up the weapon they needed to get to many more Super Bowls—and that was speed."

Instead of utilizing that advantage, however, the Cowboys went for the pass on third down and appeared to make the correct call when Smith broke free in the end zone. However, instead of securing the ball to tie the score, Smith dropped the apparently easy touchdown. "I just missed it," Smith said. "It was a great call. I was trying to get down with the ball because it was a little low, but as I got down I lost my footing. I couldn't get the right position, and my feet ended up in front of me. I think the ball hit my hip instead of my chest. It's hard to remember. It just might have been a matter of being overcautious."

After that play, Dallas place-kicker Rafael Septien ended up booting a 27-yard field goal that made it 21-17, but the Cowboys would have tied the score with a Smith touchdown. The kick ended up being the only third-quarter score, and Dallas never got any closer.

"I was kind of in the area, but the question was—and I don't think it was ever resolved—who was supposed to be covering him," Wagner said. "What was really interesting about the Cowboys is that they ran that play, and we were very confused on defense. Jackie was so wide open, but I think his foot slipped a little bit to cause him to misplay that ball.

"And that's really unfortunate, because he was such a great player. But quite honestly, our line of thinking was that even if he had caught that ball . . . there was a lot of football to be played. And a lot more plays could happen. Our defense, we really didn't talk about it after that, but the amazing thing was that the Cowboys didn't run that play again."

Fr. Sean said he felt badly for Smith, noting that he "seemed like one of the last people on the Cowboys that you would want that to happen to, but it was great for the Steelers."

The Steelers quickly took advantage on their next possession, and they were the beneficiary of a controversial pass-interference call. After moving to their 44-yard line, Bradshaw attempted a pass to Swann, but the wideout collided with Dallas defensive back Benny Barnes and a penalty was called on the cornerback. It could have been incidental contact, but the penalty gave Pittsburgh a first down at Dallas' 23-yard line. Two plays later, the Steelers faced a third-and-4 situation from the Dallas 17. Henderson sacked Bradshaw for a 12-yard loss, but the play was nullified by a delay-of-game penalty on Pittsburgh, making it third-and-9, instead of fourth down. Replays clearly showed that most Dallas players pulled up after a whistle sounded, but Henderson claimed he didn't hear it. Steelers running back Franco Harris confronted Henderson for tackling Bradshaw after the whistle; and on the next play, he blasted through the Cowboys for a 22-yard touchdown run to give the Steelers a 28-17 lead.

Gerela slipped on the ensuing kickoff, and the ball bounced to Cowboys lineman Randy White at the 24-yard line. White, who was playing the game with a cast on his broken left hand, fumbled the ball just before being hit by Steelers safety Tony Dungy. Linebacker Dennis "Dirt" Winston recovered the ball at the Dallas 18-yard line. On the next play, Bradshaw threw an 18-yard touchdown pass to Swann to increase Pittsburgh's lead to 35-17 with less than seven minutes remaining in the game.

On their next drive, the Cowboys drove 89 yards in eight plays to score on Staubach's seven-yard touchdown pass to Dupree. After Dallas safety Dennis Thurman recovered an onside kick, Pearson caught passes for 22 and 25 yards, respectively, as the Cowboys drove another 52 yards. Staubach's four-yard touchdown pass to wideout Butch Johnson cut the score to 35-31 with just 22 seconds remaining, but there the score would remain.

Swann was the leading receiver in the game with seven receptions for 124 yards and a touchdown, while Stallworth tallied 115 yards and a touchdown on just three receptions. They became the first wideout duo to reach 100-plus receiving yards in the Super Bowl.

Super Bowl XIII assembled the greatest collection of NFL talent ever to gather for a game. In addition to Landry and Steelers head coach Chuck Noll, 14 players would go on to be enshrined in the Pro Football Hall of Fame: Steelers Bradshaw, Harris, Swann, Stallworth, Greene, Blount, center Mike Webster, middle linebacker Jack Lambert, and outside linebacker Jack Ham, and Cowboys Staubach, Dorsett, White, Jackie Smith, and right offensive tackle Rayfield Wright. Dungy, of course, went on to coach the Indianapolis Colts to victory in Super Bowl XLI, becoming just the third person in NFL history—along with Mike Ditka and Tom Flores—to win Super Bowls as a player and a head coach.

"The two best teams in football met (in the Super Bowl), and the best team won," Harris said.

Wagner agreed.

"We had a great team and so did the Cowboys," Wagner said. "We had a great defense and an offense that improved from our first two Super Bowls because we had a good passing attack to go with our strong running game."

Just like Fr. Sean Francis, that big change made the big difference.

10

THE DOOR REMAINS CLOSED

1979 AFC Championship Game
Three Rivers Stadium
Pittsburgh, Pennsylvania
January 6, 1980

BOB FRITZKY WAS BORN AND RAISED in the Pittsburgh area, about three miles from the city in the Crafton-Ingram area, and graduated from nearby Canevin Catholic High School and Duquesne University before business took him to several stops around the country late in 1982.

Fritzky remained connected to Pittsburgh—thanks to his nearly 90-year-old mother, Irene, who has maintained a home there, and the Steelers—despite setting up residences at times in Chicago, Columbus, Indianapolis, Chicago again, New Jersey, and currently Moraga, California, about 17 miles from San Francisco. Two stints in Chicago, however, made him a Bears fan as well.

"They're in the NFC, so I justified it that way," Fritzky said. "But I still live and die with the black and gold. Along with my mother, I had two aunts that had a strong influence on me. They helped raise me and strengthened my love for the Steelers."

Fritzky's father passed away in 1961, when he was five, so his mother and aunts, Margaret and Mary Tucnik, got him interested in the Steelers. Margaret, who lived on the North Side close to Three Rivers Stadium, usually scored tickets to Steelers home games from her company for Fritzky and his brother. The two attended at least a couple games a year once they were in their teens. The two went to both AFC playoff games in 1972 and nearly left before Franco Harris' Immaculate Reception that beat the Oakland Raiders. But they decided to stay and got to see one of the most exciting plays in NFL history. It actually was voted the No. 1 play of all time.

The Steelers lost the next week to the Miami Dolphins, who completed an undefeated season with a Super Bowl victory against the Washington Redskins, even though many on the Steelers believed they were better than the champions. Though they had another good regular season in 1973, they were ousted by the Raiders in the previous year's playoffs. But that just made the Steelers even hungrier in 1974.

"I'll never forget that season," Fritzky said. "There was a lot of interest in the Steelers, because of the previous two seasons, and they ended up playing pretty well after a slow start. They really came together down the stretch, and they dominated in the playoffs.

"And I'll always remember that first Super Bowl against the Minnesota Vikings. It was so intense, a great game, a great defensive game on both sides. The offenses struggled to move the ball, but the Steelers ran the ball well with Franco in the second half. And their defense was great."

Fritzky was in college at Duquesne as the Steelers tried to win back-to-back Super Bowls for the second time in six years—four in six seasons overall—while Pittsburgh worked itself into a frenzy about its sports teams. The Pirates won the 1979 World Series in October, just as the Steelers were forging another playoff run, and Pittsburgh became known as the City of Champions.

"What a great time for sports fans in Pittsburgh," Fritzky recalled.

The Steelers were 6-2 at midseason in 1979 after a 42-7 blowout win against the Denver Broncos at Three Rivers Stadium and followed that with a tough 14-3 decision against the Dallas Cowboys at home as well. They also beat the Washington Redskins 38-7 at home and pounded the Kansas City Chiefs 30-3 on the road. During that four-game winning streak to run their record to 9-2, the Steelers outscored the opposition 124-20. The Steelers went 3-2 in the final five games, but tuned up for the playoffs with a 28-0 win against the Buffalo Bills in the regular-season finale.

"We were playing pretty well on offense and defense that season," Steelers defensive end Dwight White said. "We were known as more of a defensive-oriented team during our earlier Super Bowl runs, but our offense really came together after that. And in 1978 and '79, we were really playing well on both sides of the ball. That's what made us so tough to beat."

The Steelers gave up an average of about 16 points per game, while scoring an even 26 to rank among the league-leaders, and they outscored their opponents 416-262. Bradshaw completed nearly 55 percent of his passes for more than 3,700 yards, by far his best NFL season, and threw 26 touchdown passes with 25 interceptions. Those last two figures were usually close, but he liked to throw the ball around the field. Harris ran for 1,186 yards, his second-best NFL season, and scored 11 touchdowns. While John Stallworth led the Steelers with 70 receptions for nearly 1,200 yards and eight touchdowns, Lynn Swann and tight end Bennie Cunningham added 41 and 36 catches, respectively. Harris also caught 36 passes out of the backfield. Stallworth's reception total was the best in his career until he snared 75 catches in 1985. He pretty much was overshadowed by Swann to this point, but he was every bit as productive.

The Steelers walloped the Miami Dolphins in an AFC divisional playoff game, 34-14, at Three Rivers Stadium to set up a matchup with the Houston Oilers in the AFC title game for the second straight season. The Oilers were led by flamboyant head coach O.A. "Bum" Phillips, a good ole boy who was a favorite of fans and players alike around the league. Phillips had the Oilers playing well, and they had beaten the Steelers just a few weeks earlier, 20-17, in the Astrodome. That game was surrounded by a controversial call on an onside kick. The Steelers thought they had the ball with a shot to tie the game on a field goal, but the officials ruled against them. The AFC title game, however, would be at Three Rivers Stadium, which rarely was a hospitable host for the southern-based Oilers.

"They never did too well in Pittsburgh," Steelers safety Mike Wagner recalled. "And even though they were pretty competitive with us, we always believed we were better than them. And we certainly beat them enough times to back that up. It wasn't being cocky, but it was just how we felt."

White quickly agreed. The Oilers players were used to playing games indoors at the Astrodome and in warm weather, White said. So, they never knew what they were getting into and never seemed to be prepared. White also noted that the Steelers always believed they could beat the Oilers in any situation and were especially confident after the serious butt-kicking they put on them in the AFC title game the previous season.

Sam Ross Jr., the Steelers beat writer for the *Tribune-Democrat* in Johnstown, Pennsylvania, believed that the Oilers were more confident this season.

"I don't know why, for sure," Ross Jr. said. "Maybe it was because they won that game in Houston; but from Phillips to the players they really thought they had a chance to finally beat the Steelers that year."

Past records really didn't mean anything to the Oilers, and Phillips preached that this finally would be his team's season to "kick in that steel door" and get past the Steelers in the playoffs—an admirable belief by the loquacious coach, but easier said than done on the football field. The Steelers made certain that was the case this time around as well, even though they trailed from the outset when Vernon Perry picked off Steelers quarterback Terry Bradshaw inside the Houston 30 and returned it an AFC championship game-record 75 yards for a touchdown. The two teams traded field goals after that, a 21-yarder by Steelers place-kicker Matt Bahr and 27-yarder by Houston's Toni Fritsch, and the Oilers held a 10–3 advantage midway through the second quarter. That's when Bradshaw and the Steelers offense—and the defense—really got hot.

The Steelers defense held Houston running back Earl Campbell—the NFL's leading rusher with nearly 1,700 yards that season—to a measly 15 yards on 17 carries. Steelers defensive tackle Joe Greene slashed through cracks in Houston's offensive line and nailed Campbell for lost yardage. The plays were made possible when Greene moved around along the line and set himself to either side of

Houston's center. Then, he just used his quickness and strength to fire between the center and guard to make a play in the backfield. Not only did plays like that fire up the Steelers defense, they got the team's offense going as well.

"That happened a lot," Steelers running back Rocky Bleier said. "Sure, we could move the ball down the field by the pass or the run that season, but we had a lot of short fields thanks to our defense. They were a real dominant group, and Joe Greene had just a monster game against the Oilers."

Bleier wasn't too bad, either, with 13 carries for 52 yards, solid blocking for Harris' 85 yards on 21 carries and three receptions for 39 additional yards. Bradshaw had an average day with 18-for-30 passing for 219 yards, but his two second-quarter touchdown connections were huge. He hit tight end Bennie Cunningham for a 16-yarder and hooked up with Stallworth from 20 yards out to give the Steelers a 17-10 advantage at halftime. The score remained that way through a scoreless third quarter, but the Oilers were on the verge of tying it late in that stanza.

"The game was pretty close, to that point, just like the one in Houston a few weeks earlier," Wagner said. "It could have gone either way, but we were a pretty confident bunch. We beat them pretty badly in Pittsburgh early in the season (38-7 in the second week), and we definitely thought we could beat them again."

Houston quarterback Dan Pastorini, just as flamboyant as his head coach, guided the Oilers into the red zone and appeared to be poised to score the tying touchdown. Pastorini, who played a gutsy game with 19-for-28 passing for 203 yards despite getting harassed by the Steelers defense the entire game, lofted a pass into the corner of the end zone for wideout Mike Renfro. He deftly pulled in the pass and then fell out of play despite having Steelers rookie cornerback Ron Johnson basically on his back the entire time. But there was some question whether Renfro caught the pass inbounds or if he even had control before falling out.

This is the type of game that would just drive Bob Fritzky nuts. Described by his wife, Jeanette, as an ornery fan, Fritzky can get so intense and uptight when the Steelers are losing or in a tight game—

103

such as this one against the Oilers—that Jeanette makes him turn off the television. For the sake of the household and their marriage, Jeanette says, it's best that Fritzky doesn't watch any big games.

"I could hardly breathe during the Super Bowl run in 2005," Fritzky said. "I think I take after my mother. She hasn't changed at all over the years. She still gets fired up while watching the Steelers."

Irene Fritzky's intensity and love for the Steelers followed her son his entire life. When he moved away from Pittsburgh, Fritzky said he couldn't wait to open the newspaper on Friday to see the weekend TV listings to find out if the Steelers would be on TV in his area. Nowadays, he mostly gets West Coast teams, but really can't deal with watching them. Fritzky said he ends up pulling out his cell phone to follow the Steelers in-game progress that way, watches a "meaningless game" to view the scores flashing on the screen or watches ESPN to follow the sports ticker at the bottom of the screen to get updates. None are optimal options for Fritzky, but it's what he has had to deal with since moving from Western Pennsylvania.

"I also call my mother every day, especially during football season, to find out what's going on with the Steelers," Fritzky said. "She follows the team very closely and lets me know the latest news."

Jeanette and Bob Fritzky have four children—Zac and Lindsay, who are in their mid-20s, and near-teenage twins Patrick and Ann. They're all Steelers fans, but the twins are the most fervent and even wear team jerseys to school, which brings some heat from their friends in the Bay Area. Zac has also liked the New Orleans Saints, Fritzky said, since they were the "Aints." Lindsay is a fair-weather football fan and watches the Steelers more often when they're winning. Fritzky still tries to secure team gear, jerseys, Terrible Towels and the like, for his children.

Fritzky even decided to go to the Steelers road game against the Oakland Raiders in 2006 even though it was against Jeanette's wishes. She feared that he might get beaten up for wearing a Steelers jersey. His compromise was to wear a black turtleneck and just cheer for the Steelers, although there wasn't much to be happy about in that game, as quarterback Ben Roethlisberger threw several interceptions, including two that were returned for touchdowns—

COURTESY OF THE FRITZKY FAMILY

The Fritzky Fan Club includes father Bob Fritzky, son Patrick, daughter Ann, and dogs Balto and Asian.

and one of those was run back 100 yards for a score in a heartbreaking loss.

"It was a tough game to watch," Fritzky said. "I got there about 90 minutes before the game and still had to park a mile away. There were a few other Steelers fans that day; not a lot, but we were pretty loud. I really didn't take too much abuse during the game, but the Steelers fans just didn't have a lot to cheer about."

The same thing could have been said about the Steelers' AFC title game against the Oilers after the 1979 season. Renfro caught Pastorini's pass, that's certain, but side judge Donald Orr—the official closest to the play—was unsure and looked for help. His hesitation spoke loudly to the Oilers, and then he signaled no catch and no touchdown.

"It's a shame he froze," Houston center Carl Mauck said afterward. "He didn't say it was good. Then, he said it was no good and (added) that they had to confer. I told [the ref] he didn't have the guts to make the call."

Officials got together for a little conference, then they finally made a call. The head official announced that Renfro did not have possession before he rolled out of bounds. Several plays later, the Oilers had to settle for a 23-yard Fritsch field goal. It actually happened early in the fourth quarter and got them within four, 17–13, but any momentum gained was clearly lost; and the Steelers were ready to take full advantage.

"They were wrong," Renfro said, and instant replays on the sequence appeared to confirm the Houston wideout's version. But there was still some doubt, and nothing else mattered after that.

"The Oilers were a very good team, and a lot of people believed that the Oilers got hosed," said Sam Ross Jr. "And, I guess, they did because replays showed that Renfro was inbounds. There was still some uncertainty, though.

"And that touchdown only would have tied the score, but it definitely changed the game. There was no recourse for the Oilers, because there was no instant replay in the NFL at that time. There was a lot of unhappiness over that call, and it really changed the flow in that game."

Wagner wasn't near the play, but he acknowledged that it was too close to call. Wagner, like other Steelers, noted that the score only would have been tied if the Oilers would have scored a touchdown and kicked the extra point in that situation. There was still an entire quarter to play, and Houston just didn't get the job done during that time. In fact, the Steelers owned the fourth quarter, scoring 10 more points on a 39-yard field goal by Bahr and a four-yard touchdown run by Bleier.

It seemed like the Steelers had won the Oilers' respect again, and Phillips even praised them.

"This football game was won by the Steelers," Phillips said. "They're a fine football team, and I wish them all the luck in the world in the Super Bowl. They represent our conference, so we're proud of anything they do."

Steelers safety J. T. Thomas probably said it the best after the game against Houston, recalling what an old college roommate used to say.

"We may be impersonated, but we cannot be duplicated," Thomas said after pondering for a moment. "Before us there were none, and after us there will be no more."

The Steelers would move on to their fourth Super Bowl in six years and whip the Los Angeles Rams 31–19 to win for the fourth time as well. No other team had matched that success rate to this point, and none are likely to ever win four times in six years. The Steelers were the best team in the NFL again, the undisputed team of the decade in the 1970s, and secured a spot among the NFL's all-time teams with one dynamic performance.

And that steel door would forever stay shut on the Houston Oilers.

11

FATE, BUT NO DIVINE INTERVENTION

Super Bowl XIV
Rose Bowl
Pasadena, California
January 20, 1980

YOUNG SARAH CROTTY AND HER FAMILY moved around a lot in her formative years, as her father's various jobs took them to Cincinnati and Atlanta and places in Kentucky and Michigan, but football was a constant.

With strong mentoring from her father and older brother, Tom, Sarah developed a fondness for NFL games. Tom matriculated to the University of Michigan, so the Crottys attended football games there, but Sarah already was a big Pro Football fan. Then fate intervened in 1975.

Sarah's father, an executive for Rockwell International in Michigan, was promoted to an office at the company's Pittsburgh headquarters. So Patrick and Helen Crotty packed up their family and moved that summer. Older siblings Colleen, Tom, Mary, and Liz were already out of the house, and Sarah would have to spend her freshman year in high school in Pittsburgh.

Little did Sarah know that she would spend the better part of her life in the area, become a Catholic nun—Sister Sarah, CSSJ (the Congregation of the Sisters of St. Joseph)—and a Steelers season ticket holder. That's jumping ahead just a bit, but Sarah definitely didn't know how dramatically her life would change after that August in 1975.

Gerald Ford was the president of the United States. Several Watergate conspirators were found guilty and sentenced to prison terms. The No. 1 record was "I Honestly Love You," by Olivia Newton-John. *The Godfather, Part II* won the Academy Award for Best Picture, and the Pittsburgh Steelers captured the franchise's first Super Bowl.

The Steelers became just the second team to win back-to-back Super Bowl titles after the 1975 season, Sarah's freshman year at Vincentian, an all-girls Catholic high school in the area, and she fit in perfectly with the other kids. She was athletic, so she could play basketball and field hockey there, and the Steelers quickly became Sarah's favorite NFL team.

"Being a new kid in a new town, well, I always say that the Steelers gave me a hometown," Sarah said. "Before that, we had moved a lot, so I always felt like I wasn't from anywhere. But when we moved to Pittsburgh, the bonding and binding thing for me was the Steelers and how much this town loves them. It still amazes me.

"I remember before we moved to Pittsburgh we looked for houses in the area, I couldn't believe that every house had black and gold colors in it somewhere. It was incredible. My Dad's a rabid football fan, so I grew up watching it, and it was kind of a way for me to bond with him. And we always loved watching the Steelers."

Sarah noted that since Vincentian didn't have a football team, the girls basically adopted the Steelers as their team. They had black-and-gold days at school and wore the team's colors on the Friday before games during football season. Jack Lambert and John Stallworth were Sarah's two favorite Steelers. She even had a No. 82 Stallworth jersey and a Steelers scarf.

And that last item has an interesting story to go along with it.

"We were at this one game at Three Rivers Stadium, a very cold day, and I was drinking hot chocolate," Sarah said. "John Stallworth made a great catch for a touchdown, and I spilled my hot chocolate on that scarf. To this day, I haven't washed that scarf. That's kinda gross, but it was good luck."

Steelers wideout John Stallworth elevated his game in Super Bowl XIV.

Occasionally, through corporate connections, Patrick Crotty secured Steelers tickets. And Sarah remembers going to running back Rocky Bleier's last game. "I think it was against the Kansas City Chiefs," she said. But she watched every game on television and collected everything she could about the two-time Super Bowl champion Steelers. In fact, Sarah still has the *Sports Illustrated* that sported Super Bowl X MVP Lynn Swann on the cover.

The Steelers lost in the playoffs the next two seasons, but they came back to win Super Bowl XIII against the Dallas Cowboys, as Terry Bradshaw earned MVP honors with a great performance.

Lynn Swann and Stallworth both had big games, as the Steelers built a big lead before holding on to win 35-31.

"That was my senior year, and it was great," Sarah said. "But the next year, 1979, my Dad's job took him to Los Angeles. I didn't have any college plans at that point, so I went with him. And we got tickets to Super Bowl XIV at the Rose Bowl there. It was an unbelievable experience."

That's mostly because the Steelers were there as well. They qualified by going 12-4 in the regular season and winning the AFC Central Division. The Steelers pounded Miami (34-14) and Houston (27-13) in the playoffs and met the "hometown" Los Angeles Rams, the NFC champions, for the Super Bowl title in front of a record crowd of 103,985.

The opponents could not have been more contrasting. The Steelers, of course, were making their fourth Super Bowl appearance in six seasons. For the Rams, it was their first, but it capped their seventh consecutive NFC Western Division title. It also marked the first time an NFC West team had qualified for the title game, but the Rams' 9-7 record was the poorest of any Super Bowl team. They edged out the New Orleans Saints by just one game to win the NFC West and beat Tampa Bay in the NFC championship game 9-0 on three Frank Corral field goals.

Bradshaw was entrenched as the Steelers signal-caller, but the Rams had a quarterback controversy. Third-year pro Vince Ferragamo emerged down the stretch in the regular season to replace injured Pat Haden. He suffered a broken finger. Rookie Jeff Rutledge from Alabama and veteran Bob Lee also took some snaps before Ferragamo recovered from a broken hand to take control and guiding the Rams to a 6-1 mark down the stretch.

There was a contrast in the head coaches, as well, with the Steelers being guided by steely Charles Henry Noll, while the Rams were led by Raymondo Giuseppi Giovanni Baptiste Malavasi. Ray Malavasi had replaced George Allen midway through the preseason schedule in 1978 after a checkered career that started at Fort Belvoir, Virginia, while he was in military service. He was an assistant coach at the University of Minnesota, Memphis State, and Wake Forest before being hired as personnel director of the Denver Broncos in 1962.

In 1966, following the dismissal of Mac Speedie, Malavasi coached the Broncos to a 4-8 record. He was defensive coordinator of the Hamilton Tiger-Cats of the Canadian Football League the following year. In 1969, he became an assistant with the Buffalo Bills, moved to the Oakland Raiders as an assistant in 1970 and joined the Rams in 1973, serving as defensive coordinator under Coach Chuck Knox. For Allen, he was offensive coordinator and offensive coach. Malavasi underwent quadruple bypass heart surgery early in 1978. A year later, in the spring of 1979, he was hospitalized for treatment of hypertension and he was still on medication during the Super Bowl and likely needed it to be controlled during a seesaw game.

The Steelers opened the scoring with a field goal by rookie Matt Bahr from Penn State, but Rams bruising fullback Cullen Bryant plowed in from the 1 later in the first quarter for a 7-3 advantage. Bahr's short kickoff gave the Rams good field position, and starting tailback Wendell Tyler set up the score with a 39-yard run. Franco Harris regained the lead for the Steelers with a second-quarter score on a one-yard run, as Bradshaw needed just nine plays to take them down the field after Larry Anderson returned the kickoff 45 yards. It was one of five kickoffs he returned that day for a Super Bowl-record 162 yards, but the lead was short-lived. Corral field goals from 31 and 45 yards gave the Rams a 13-10 edge at halftime.

"It was an uneasy feeling; that's for sure," Steelers defensive end Dwight White said. "We knew we could win the game, but we also knew that we'd have to make some adjustments. Really, we never thought we were going to lose, but it was going to be a test of maturity and character."

The Steelers moved the ball well, especially in their passing game, but Bradshaw threw three interceptions to keep Los Angeles in the game. He was able to connect with Swann for a 47-yard touchdown early in the third quarter to give the Steelers the lead again, 17-13. Rams free safety Nolan Cromwell appeared to have position to pick off the pass or at least knock it down, but he mistimed his leap and the ball sailed over his head to Swann.

Once again, the lead for the Steelers would not last long. The Rams moved the length of the field and scored another touchdown in only four plays. A 50-yard pass from Rams quarterback Vince Ferragamo to wideout Billy Waddy moved them to the Steelers 24. The Rams regained the lead with some trickery, as backup running back Lawrence McCutcheon took a handoff and fired into the end zone to backup wideout Ron Smith to make it 19-17, but the Rams would miss the extra point.

The circumstances were dire, but the Steelers weren't finished with the entire fourth quarter ahead, Bradshaw embracing a gunslinger mentality and the most talented pair of big-play receivers in the league on their side. At 2:56 into the final quarter, after the score had already changed hands five times, it was third-and-eight with the Steelers on their own 27. The play was known as "60 prevent, slot, hook and go," and Bradshaw dropped back to pass and looked downfield for one of those athletic wideouts.

Swann, already a Steelers hero for his MVP performance in Super Bowl X against Dallas, came across the middle on a short route that would have resulted in a first down if completed. Stallworth, the slot receiver, took two defenders about 15 yards downfield, hooked, and then went deep.

Almost from the moment he was selected by the Steelers, Stallworth was the other kid on the block, the wide receiver who gained recognition only if some spilled over from the more-heralded Swann. In the 1974 draft, Swann was selected No. 1 by the Steelers, while Stallworth was taken in the fourth round. A product of small Alabama A&M, Stallworth was hardly a publicity match for Swann, who was an All-American from powerhouse Southern Cal. Stallworth was the club's workhorse receiver, while Swann was more of an acrobatic artist whose very name implied ballet-like grace.

Along with his performance in Super Bowl X, Swann had a terrific game in Super Bowl XIII against Dallas again. Stallworth caught two first-half touchdown passes against the Cowboys in that latter game, but he basically sat out the second half with serious leg cramps and again was overshadowed by Swann. It seemed like the spotlight always averted from Stallworth and shined brightly on

Young Sarah Crotty poses with her copy of the program from Super Bowl XIV in Los Angeles.

Swann. But Stallworth redirected it a bit during the 1979 season when he set a Steelers record with 70 catches for 1,183 yards despite suffering from two sprained wrists that made it too painful for him to lift his infant daughter during the season.

Maybe that season and this championship game would finally put Stallworth in the same class as Swann, Steelers hero and Super Bowl MVP.

"The game was just unbelievable through three quarters," Sarah said. "It was so exciting, and I still vividly remember everything. The Steelers fans at the game were going wild. You know, Los Angeles has about eight zillion people, but I don't think they have a lot of football fans because everything seemed to be black and gold for the two weeks leading up to the Super Bowl."

Sarah fit right in. She was dressed in Steelers colors from head to toe, just like she does for games to this day. And Sarah is prepared for any situation. She has warm-weather black and gold clothes, like she wore to Super Bowl XIV, and cold-weather gear that she wears on Sunday's at Heinz Field. Her wardrobe consists of Steelers

115

hats, sweatshirts, and gloves, and don't forget, she still has that lucky scarf.

Her father, Patrick, was just fortunate to be at the Super Bowl at all. He was injured in a fall and broke six ribs in his back over the Christmas holiday, but he still attended the game. Sarah said he ignored the pain and cheered and yelled for the Steelers just like always. So they both were part of the large Steelers contingent that Sarah said seemed to be as much as 80 percent black and gold.

Sarah has had season tickets since the club moved to Heinz Field in 2001 and hasn't missed a game since. She and a friend, attorney Patty Blais, attend the games together to cheer for the Steelers. And when she's back with the other nuns in residence at St. Titus in Aliquippa, the football talk doesn't stop.

"I think you can talk football with anyone around here, especially women," Sarah said. "That's the hometown part of it. I think the women around here know as much about football as anyone. They might not be big sports fans, but they're certainly Steelers fans. And they're very serious about them."

For those who know Sister Sarah personally or at her job as a social worker for Focus on Renewal in Slippery Rock, they might not recognize her at a Steelers game. She doesn't go through a complete transformation, cursing and drinking beer, but she gets into the games for sure.

"I'm pretty loud at the games," Sarah said. "I usually have a voice problem the day after a Steelers game, but that's about it. But I must confess, I never pray for the Steelers to win. As much as I love my boys it just doesn't seem right with all the other needs in the world."

Sarah added that she isn't opposed to a priest mentioning the Steelers during a Sunday mass since the club is a large part of their fans' lives. Talk to anyone at a game or in a bar on a Sunday during football season. In Western Pennsylvania, that season starts in July at training camp and runs into January and hopefully February and the Super Bowl. And don't forget the NFL Draft in April, as well as mini-camp and the spring workouts.

"When the Steelers take the field and all the Terrible Towels are waving, it's beautiful," Sarah said. "Each time I go to the stadium for a game, regular season or not, my heart starts pounding and I get all excited. Doesn't everyone think black and gold are the most beautiful colors in the world?"

That certainly was the case for the thousands of pro-Steelers fans in attendance during Super Bowl XIV, and those colors never shined brighter than they did about three minutes into the fourth quarter. Bradshaw, fate and the Super Bowl spotlight found Stallworth going deep.

Bradshaw cut loose with a long bomb that eluded cornerback Rod Perry's grasp and landed perfectly in Stallworth's arms for a stunning 73-yard touchdown that finally pushed the momentum toward the Steelers. They extended their 24-19 advantage to the final score with seven more points midway through the fourth quarter. The Rams drove into Steelers territory at the 32, but Ferragamo was picked off by Lambert. Bradshaw hooked up with Stallworth for 45 yards to change the field position, and a pass-interference penalty put the ball at the 1. Harris slammed it in from there.

Bradshaw was the MVP for completing 14 of 21 passes for 309 yards and two touchdowns, but Stallworth's day of recognition had finally arrived. The 6-foot-2 Alabama native caught three passes for 121 yards and that spectacular clinching 73-yard touchdown pass from Bradshaw. It was the deciding score during a game that was in the balance for three quarters. But the play that propelled the Steelers to their fourth Super Bowl title had been worked on constantly during the practice week before the big game. Eight times, Stallworth disclosed, and the play never worked even once.

"It's hard to have confidence in a play that never works, but I think it didn't work because the field was too soggy," Stallworth said. "Terry was throwing the ball long, and I just couldn't get to it."

Bradshaw fired deep again, but Stallworth caught up to it about 40 yards from the line of scrimmage. He bolted the remaining 30-plus yards for the touchdown. It was as graceful a play as any that Swann had made, and it was just as crucial to the Steelers' success.

"Usually, on that play, the receiver hooks and slides," Bradshaw said. "And that's the way that the Rams defended it. But Stallworth took it to the next level, and we got the big touchdown. I didn't know if it would work. I don't think it worked at all in practice, but it worked later in the game, too."

Bradshaw and Stallworth hooked up for a 45-yard gain the second time, and that set up the final score by Harris.

"I felt all along that I could deliver the big play," Stallworth said. "I felt like I could go deep on anybody in the NFL. We tried to beat them with the bomb and go deep on the fly pattern because they were double-covering short and deep. And they were looking mostly for Swanny."

After winning four Super Bowls in six seasons in the 1970s, the Steelers followers expected recognition as the Team of the Decade. They also should have been ranked among the best teams of all-time in the NFL. Just ask beloved owner Art Rooney Sr.

"This might be the greatest team of all time," Mr. Rooney said after the game, a large cigar in his mouth and Vince Lombardi Trophy in his hands. "I'm proud of my boys. These are the most gentlemanly fellows I've ever had. None of the team gets swell-headed."

Noll rarely commented on that topic, but even he believed the Steelers Super Bowl XIV win was the team's best performance in an amazing run. Ubiquitous linebacker Jack Ham agreed, mostly because the club was so well-rounded. The Steelers could beat an opponent with their stifling defense, but they also had developed a big-play offense as well.

"Comparisons are hard to make, but I think we're the greatest," Ham said. "The No. 1 factor is depth. We have 45 players who can play. We have much more depth than we have ever had. And we can win a lot of different ways. We can grind it out and make all the big plays."

Cornerback Mel Blount believed this victory put the Steelers at a different level compared to the rest of the NFL.

"Winning a fourth Super Bowl should put us in a special category," Blount said. "I think this is the best team ever assembled. They talk about Vince Lombardi, but I think the Chuck Noll era is even greater."

Few Steelers demonstrated more elation with the victory than defensive back J. T. Thomas. He had been sidelined the entire 1978 season with a blood disorder and missed Super Bowl XIII. He recovered in time to play again in 1979 and got one more Super Bowl ring.

"It's something I wished for, hoped for and prayed for," Thomas said. "I think we can be imitated, but I don't think we can be duplicated. We knew that the best way for them to win the game was for us to beat ourselves.

"But we didn't. We win together as a team. We lose together, and we screw up together. The difference between us and the Rams is that they only thought they could beat us, but we knew we could beat them."

Not only could the Steelers lay claim to being a dynasty with four Super Bowl titles in six seasons as the proof, Bradshaw could be ranked among the game's best as well. He was a Super Bowl MVP for the second straight year, the second repeat winner, as quarterback Bart Starr did the same for the Green Bay Packers in Super Bowls I and II in 1967 and '68. He also became the Super Bowl leader with nine touchdown passes and 932 passing yards.

"They were the all-time best, there's no question," Sarah said. "The players on those Super Bowl teams, they were great. "We might never see a team like that again."

Unless, of course, fate intervenes for the Steelers.

12

OUT WITH A BANG

Bradshaw's Last Game
Shea Stadium
New York, New York
December 10, 1983

FEW THINGS ARE MORE ROMANTIC to a woman than returning to the site where she got engaged, so Ed Schuessler used that to his advantage and also combined his two loves in the process by getting engaged to girlfriend Becky Skelton at a Pittsburgh Steelers NFL game.

Schuessler, known as Iron City Ed the past few years—ICE, for short—for his dedication to the Steelers, chose December 20, 1992 as the big day. It was coach Bill Cowher's first season, and the Steelers played the Minnesota Vikings at Three Rivers Stadium with the top spot in the AFC playoffs up for grabs. That wasn't uppermost on Schuessler's mind. Not much, anyway, as he set the plans in motion for the proposal earlier that week.

"I was in contact with the Steelers public relations people, and they told me the announcement would be on the scoreboard right at the end of the third quarter," Schuessler said. "So I waited the whole game for that."

The game wasn't too exciting otherwise and ended in a 6-3 Vikings victory, but Schuessler was getting pumped for his big moment. He even was able to improve their seating to a section on the 50-yard line to get a better scoreboard view. But just before the third quarter ended and Schuessler began his elaborate proposal, Becky decided to take a bathroom break.

"I couldn't believe it and told her to hold off for a while because the line would be too long at the end of the quarter," Schuessler said.

Schuessler spent the next few minutes prepping Becky for the big moment, talking about how long they've been together and pledging his love for her, and then the message appeared on the scoreboard: "Becky, I love you. Will you marry me? Ed." Schuessler called Becky's attention to it and mentioned how interesting that two people with their same names were going to get engaged. Then, he pulled out a camera to immortalize the moment.

"I have it blown up and put on my wall now," Schuessler said. "Becky eventually said yes, but I had a deal. 'Now, honey,' I said, 'we have to go back once a year to celebrate.' And I've been back for at least one game a year."

Thus, he pulled Becky into his life with the Steelers. Not unwillingly, it should be added, but into it quite deeply nonetheless. But that's the way it should be, Schuessler noted. Sure, Becky might not understand all the rules, but she happily goes to the games, tailgates, and has a great time like any good Steelers fan. Ed was born and raised in Central Illinois, and the Schuesslers reside in Collinsville, Illinois, now, about 15 miles east of St. Louis. But Ed's summers spent with his father and grandmother in Mount Oliver, on Pittsburgh's South Side, produced and developed his love for the Steelers.

Schuessler, now 44, spent part of the summer in his youth watching heroes like Roberto Clemente and Willie Stargell play for the Pirates at Forbes Field, collecting Topps football and baseball cards and pining for football season to arrive. By his own admission, Schuessler was a hardcore fan since the time the Steelers went on their initial Super Bowl runs in the early 1970s. He stayed with them, as any true fan would, he noted, during the more difficult 1980s and got his first satellite dish in 1995 in time to view the Steelers return to the top in the NFL in Super Bowl XXX.

Schuessler has been to many Steelers games over the years, in Pittsburgh—in accordance with his agreement with Becky in

1992—as well as on the road. And he has watched countless more on television. He also has become quite a collector. Schuessler has a memorabilia room, "basically a Steelers Hall of Fame," he said, in his basement. Items on display include autographs from his favorite players and photos, including the classic one from the Three Rivers Stadium scoreboard when he proposed to Becky. That has a prominent spot in Schuessler's Steelers room. There's also a large banner proclaiming "You're In Steelers Country" on the basement wall.

The Schuessler's two daughters, Claire, eight years old, and Carlie, six, have also been to games. Claire, the family tomboy, plays basketball, baseball, and soccer. And she told her father that she would like to play linebacker for the Steelers when she gets older. Dad said she needs to gain a little weight and work on her quickness, but she's certainly tough enough. Carlie has vowed to start the first Steelers cheerleading squad after she noticed that there were none at a game the family attended a few years ago.

On Sundays during football season, Ed and Becky have 6-10 rabid Steelers fans at their home to watch the games in his black-and-gold themed basement. As night falls, they can see a projection on a side of his house that reads: "Here We Go Steelers, Here We Go." Those who will attend the Steelers 2007 game at St. Louis against the Rams might get to see Schuessler's Steelers Hall of Fame room or just hear about it, but it's certain that they'll all have many stories to share after that football weekend.

In the past few years, Schuessler began to collect e-mail addresses from Steelers buddies to share information about the team. Now, he has nearly 100 names. The group includes ticket brokers, memorabilia dealers and office workers with one thing in common, a love for the Steelers. And they correspond to others like them around the country.

"It's amazing, when you think about it, how much this group has grown," Schuessler said. "But when I talk to people, I give them my business card that has a Steelers logo on it, and we just start talking.

"And one thing I know about Steelers fans is that we can sit down and talk for a long time just like we knew each other all our lives, even though we just met. My wife's amazed that I can do that. I can see someone on the street and talk to him for a while, and he's a friend for life."

One of those Steelers connections first called him Iron City Ed, and the nickname stuck. But now he just goes by the acronym Ice. Schuessler hasn't created his own Steelers Web site just yet, but corresponds on a regular basis with nearly every Steelers fan that he has met who has an e-mail address. Schuessler said that if he does get a Web site, he'll likely play off his nickname, Ice, or get involved with others who have recovered from substance abuse. Schuessler has a master's degree in social work and already is involved with helping others as an adolescent therapist and substance abuse counselor. The Web site and chat room could help other Steelers fans in need of support. To contact Schuessler, use eschu1@charter.net as an e-mail address.

"I'm really very open about it, so maybe this will inspire somebody," Schuessler said. "The kind of shape I was in from drinking and drugs, to be where I'm at right now, enjoying life. If I can do it, anybody can do it. But I just wanted to do more, so I went back to school. I truly believe that I went through what I did so that I could eventually help somebody else."

So, you still might see Schuessler at a tailgate party, talking about his favorite NFL team, but not drinking. If it's one at his home, he'll be doing the grilling. And you'll find his pet dog, a Pug named Cowher Power, there as well and dressed in his Steelers uniform. Schuessler could be wearing any one of 13 authentic jerseys he owns, either Terry Bradshaw, Lynn Swann, Franco Harris or Jack Lambert from the 1970s, Greg Lloyd, Levon Kirkland, Neil O'Donnell, or Kevin Greene from the late 1980s and 1990s or Jerome Bettis, Hines Ward, Ben Roethlisberger, or Troy Polamalu (home and away) from the more current group. He might even have a new one by then, maybe Willie Parker, Schuessler said, if it's all right with his lovely (and extremely understanding) wife, Becky.

While being clean and sober has had many advantages for Schuessler, there's one instance that stands out as far as the Steelers are concerned. Prior to a *Monday Night Football* matchup between

COURTESY OF ED AND BECKY SCHUESSLER

Steelers fans Ed and Becky Schuessler with daughters Claire and Carlie.

the Steelers and Indianapolis Colts October 21, 2002 at Heinz Field, as an alternative to tailgating, Schuessler and a friend entered the stadium early and walked through the Great Hall there. The place was relatively empty, he recalled, but one man and his family clearly stood out.

"We went in as soon as the gates opened, and the first people I saw were Terry Bradshaw and his two daughters," Schuessler said. "It was the game he returned to Pittsburgh. I really thought that this was a reward for me for not staying out in the parking lot and drinking. I got to meet my idol. I got a picture with him, and I bought his book that was called *Keep It Simple.* That was a great day for me, and I'll never forget it."

Schuessler was among those Steelers fans having a difficult time in 1983 when Cliff Stoudt attempted to replace future Hall of Famer Bradshaw as the Steelers starting quarterback. Former No. 1 pick Mark Malone also took some snaps from center, but Stoudt initially was groomed to be the heir apparent if Bradshaw could not return from an elbow injury. Malone was picked first by the Steelers in 1980, but Stoudt proved to be a better backup for Bradshaw back then. Malone also tried to play wideout for the Steelers and actually set a team record with a 90-yard touchdown catch in 1981 on his only career reception. However, he injured his knee on the play and would only play quarterback after that. So, unless Bradshaw could make a comeback, Stoudt was the man for the Steelers, at least for the moment.

Sam Ross Jr., a Steelers beat reporter for the Johnstown, Pennsylvania, *Tribune-Democrat* newspaper, remembered the season quite well.

"The Steelers got off to a good start that season, but Stoudt really wasn't playing that well overall," Ross said. "Bradshaw missed the entire season, and (wideout John) Stallworth was injured a lot that year, too. It had been a few years since the last Super Bowl, and some believed this might be the last hurrah for a while. You know, that 'One For The Thumb,' but things steadily went downhill after an early winning streak."

It was three seasons since the Steelers won their fourth Super Bowl in six years, but their only playoff appearance in the ensuing years was a loss to San Diego in the AFC Tournament following the strike-shortened 1982 season. But despite Bradshaw's injury, the Steelers opened with a 9-2 record that included a seven-game winning streak. Stoudt was an average quarterback playing pretty well in the early going, and Franco Harris was on his way to another 1,000-yard season. But things changed during the season's second half.

The Steelers lost three straight going into their December 10 game against the New York Jets at Shea Stadium. Only one regular-season game remained after that, at AFC Central Division rival Cleveland, so the game against the Jets—the NFL finale at Shea Stadium—was critical. The Steelers believed that they needed to win this game to make the playoffs. And with the growing belief that Stoudt wasn't going to get the job done, the Steelers opted to start Bradshaw at quarterback against the Jets.

"The Steelers really struggled at the end of the season and had trouble scoring," Ross said. "And Stoudt had a streak of not throwing a touchdown pass to a wide receiver. Stoudt just seemed to be fading fast in that season, and he was complaining a lot about the receivers. It wasn't a good situation."

The stage was set for the curtain to come down on Shea Stadium, at least as far as the NFL was concerned—the New York Mets would continue to play baseball there—but Bradshaw was not about to end his spectacular Steelers career with a whimper. So, he pushed the club's coaching staff to start him, even though he didn't play a down all season. And the players noticed the benefits immediately in the practices before the game.

"We've had a lot of enthusiasm in practice," Steelers tight end Bennie Cunningham would say back then. "There's no question that Terry's made a difference. I think he's got everyone on this team believing that something big was going to happen."

However, some believed that the Steelers could beat the Jets, even with Stoudt as the quarterback, but with their playoff chances tenuous at best, Bradshaw got the start.

"Bradshaw knew he shouldn't have played, but Stoudt was really struggling," Ross said. "That's why they went with Bradshaw, and he played pretty well in just a short period of time."

Bradshaw only played about 16 minutes against the Jets, and he started slowly in the Steelers' opening possession. But the second time they got the ball, Bradshaw directed them quickly downfield. He threw five passes in the eight-play drive with a 17-yard connection with rookie wide receiver Gregg Garrity ending it with a touchdown.

"It really hurt when I threw that pass to Garrity," Bradshaw said about his arm. "It was a really sharp pain. I was running right and twisted it."

It was the first NFL touchdown catch for Garrity, a hero for Penn State in their Sugar Bowl win against Georgia the year before, but it also would be the last one for his hometown team that drafted him in the fifth round that year. Garrity, a North Allegheny High School graduate, had 19 catches primarily as a possession receiver in that rookie campaign. But the Steelers did not re-sign him. He went to the other side of the state to the NFC's Philadelphia Eagles and never matched his rookie numbers in six seasons there. Garrity had 63 catches for 1,050 yards and five touchdowns with Philly. He also had a 76-yard punt return for a score, but Garrity only ran back kicks on a regular basis for one season.

Even though he was in pain, Bradshaw guided a second long drive during the Steelers' ensuing possession that spanned into the second quarter. He threw just two passes, and a 20-yard run with a reverse by wideout Greg Hawthorne moved the ball deep into Jets territory. Bradshaw's usually strong right arm was sore and started to swell after his touchdown pass to Garrity. He rolled right and fired somewhat awkwardly to the rookie, and might not have too many good throws remaining. But he still dropped back to pass after the Steelers reached the 10-yard line.

No matter what transpired from here, Bradshaw had an amazing Steelers career to this point. He was the only NFL quarterback to play in four Super Bowl victories and twice was the game's MVP. This was Bradshaw's 168th career regular-season game. He passed for nearly 28,000 yards and completed about 52 percent of his passes. Bradshaw threw nearly as many interceptions (210) as touchdowns (211) to this point, but he also had 2,257 yards rushing and 32 touchdowns on the ground.

The Steelers' No. 1 pick in 1970, as well as the NFL's top choice overall that year, Bradshaw also threw for more than 3,800 yards and 30 touchdowns with 26 interceptions in the playoffs. He ran for 288 yards and three touchdowns in the postseason as well.

Bradshaw's best games were clearly behind him and so were the Steelers', but maybe he had something left to give his team. He certainly provided a spark in the huddle for a group whose playoff hopes were fading fast. With Bradshaw back, the Steelers had a renewed confidence in their abilities and their postseason fate.

"I think we all knew we could make the playoffs, but we needed proof that we were still a good team," linebacker Loren Toews said. "Terry gave us that proof. He showed us just how good we could be. He did a heckuva job."

Cunningham believed it all started when Bradshaw first entered the huddle. The quarterback told everyone to have some fun out there, Cunningham noted, and then he proceeded to go out and lead the way.

"I knew right then that we were going places," Cunningham said. "Terry just exudes confidence, and it rubs off on everybody. Playing has been a real drudgery the past few weeks, but Bradshaw made it fun again. He just amazes me with everything he does."

And the Steelers would go just as far as Bradshaw would lead them. He already guided them to one scoring drive against the Jets and was in position for another touchdown. As Bradshaw looked into the end zone, he found wideout Calvin Sweeney open for the 10-yard score. Sweeney was drafted in the fourth round by the Steelers from Southern California in 1979, and he began an eight-year career with the club the following season. Sweeney led the Steelers with 39 catches for 577 yards and five touchdowns in 1983, but that was his best NFL season by far. Sweeney finished with 113 total receptions for 1,775 yards (a 15.7-yard average) and seven touchdowns in 102 career games that spanned eight seasons. But little did he know that the one against the Jets in that final game at Shea Stadium would be the final one in Bradshaw's career as well.

Bradshaw finished with 5-for-8 passing numbers for 77 yards and two TDs, but that would be it for him. Stoudt had to finish the game because Bradshaw severely damaged ligaments in his right (throwing) elbow, even though nobody really knew it at the time. That didn't matter, however, as the Steelers went on to win 34–7 to qualify for the AFC playoffs. But Bradshaw's career came to an abrupt end on that cold day at Shea.

The Steelers' quarterback situation was uncertain after that, as the club tried Stoudt, Malone, Bubby Brister, David Woodley, Scott Campbell, Todd Blackledge, Steve Bono, and Rick Strom before settling on Neil O'Donnell for five straight seasons. While their quarterback carousel turned after Bradshaw retired, the Steelers' on-field success spiraled downward as well.

Shea Stadium was never the same, either, as the rowdy Jets fans who remained to the end tore down both goal posts and dug up the grass field surface as the game concluded. And the NFL would never return to Shea. A year earlier, it was deemed to be too rundown and neglected and was called "the NFL's poorest facility for athletes and spectators alike," by the league, so the Jets announced plans to move to the Meadowlands in East Rutherford, New Jersey, for the 1984 season. They shared the stadium with the New York Giants and would only return to New York City if a first-class stadium was ready for occupancy, but they remain in the Meadowlands until this day. In their final season at Shea, the Jets were 7-9 and did not make the playoffs with Joe Walton as their head coach. Ironically, Walton would become the Steelers offensive coordinator just a few years later.

"It was a real mess," Ross said. "There was a drunk tank near where we were interviewing (Steelers coach Chuck) Noll. Cops kept walking past us while dragging drunks to the tank, and then we saw a cop taking a cop to that area. He tried to mace the crowd, but the wind blew it back on him.

"So he was in bad shape. Then they came back our way because they went in the wrong direction. There were drunks hanging out the bars and everything. They probably had twice as many people in there than the regular occupancy. They were jammed in there like sardines."

Despite having the crowd behind them, the Jets couldn't overcome the Steelers' quick start with Bradshaw at quarterback. So even with Stoudt under center, the Steelers kept rolling. But they were flat in a 30-17 loss at Cleveland in the regular-season finale and in a 38-10 defeat at Oakland in an AFC divisional playoff matchup. They finished 9-7 the following season, pulled an upset win at Denver in the playoffs and gave second-year quarterback Dan Marino and the Miami Dolphins a tussle before losing in the AFC title game. However, with Malone leading the way after that stunning playoff run in 1984, the Steelers' play quickly diminished.

There was just one winning season and no playoffs from 1985-88 with a 5-11 low mark in 1988 when Brister replaced Malone. The Steelers won a wild-card playoff game in 1989, but didn't make the postseason in 1990. Brister split time with O'Donnell in 1991 with no playoff appearance, and 23-year coach Chuck Noll resigned. Bill Cowher replaced him in 1992, with O'Donnell at quarterback, and that consistency led to the club's resurgence with six straight playoffs and finally another Super Bowl appearance.

But at least on that wintry day at Shea, the Steelers and Bradshaw shined, so he and the stadium went out with a bang.

13

A NEW BEGINNING

Bill Cowher's Debut
The Astrodome
Houston, Texas
September 6, 1992

JON GUNDY RECALLS the Pittsburgh Steelers glory days and four Super Bowl wins from the 1970s with great pleasure even though he's lived more than 1,000 miles away from Western Pennsylvania since 1978.

For Gundy, who was born in 1960 and raised in Beaver County, about 25 miles north of Pittsburgh, the Steelers were a large part of his life while growing up and a great way to stay connected to old friends and his roots thereafter, something that isn't likely to change any time soon.

"No, I guess I'll always be a big fan," Gundy said from his home in Cape Coral, Florida. "I remember when Chuck Noll took over, when they drafted Bradshaw, and the Immaculate Reception, of course, in 1972. I stuck with them when they were really bad in the late 1980s, and then Bill Cowher took over in 1992. I've followed them for a long time, and I probably always will."

It hasn't always been easy for Gundy, though, but not because it was tough to watch the Steelers in Noll's later years. Sure, they were really bad for a while, including a 5-11 record in 1988, but the club's games weren't always televised. When Gundy first moved to Florida in August, 1978, the Steelers were in their heyday. They already had won two Super Bowls and were on the verge of winning two more in a row.

That was a great time to be a Steelers fan, and Gundy reveled in their success. It was especially good for him since he was new to the Cape Coral area and was able to display his Steelers pride with great joy. The Gundys took some team apparel with them, including a cap, shirts, and sweatshirts, but friends from back home sent them information throughout the season and pennants, a Terrible Towel, and other championship gear during the playoffs and ensuing two Super Bowl seasons from 1978-79.

Gundy moved to Houston, Texas in 1981, while the Steelers Super Bowl teams were basically still intact, and he stayed there through 1984 before moving back to Cape Coral.

"I think the first game I saw in person was in 1975 against Kansas City (a 28-3 Steelers win)," Gundy said. "I was 15. I also saw a game in the 1980s at the Astrodome. The Steelers played the Oilers, of course. That was a good game, and the Steelers won. So it was great."

The Steelers stars from their Super Bowl teams in the 1970s were all gone by then. Terry Bradshaw retired in 1983, and Cliff Stoudt was the quarterback. Franco Harris was allowed to go to Seattle as a free agent, but Gundy remained a steadfast fan. He never stopped cheering for the Steelers, and watched them on television as much as possible.

And as satellite systems improved with NFL game packages as a feature, Gundy couldn't wait to get in on the ground floor. As a subscriber, he was able to watch every NFL game, but he never missed the Steelers.

"Before NFL Ticket came out, I went to this club in Fort Myers (which is the town next to Cape Coral on Florida's Gulf side)," Gundy said. "It was called the Players Sports Emporium, and I watched every game there."

On one particular Sunday, Gundy—dressed, as usual, in his favorite Steelers T-shirt and cap—noticed several other Steelers fans in attendance. So they started watching the games together. Meeting on Sundays during football season became a Sunday ritual, and the group began to grow with each passing week.

In 1992, William Laird Cowher was hired to replace aging legend Chuck Noll to coach the Steelers. At his opening press conference, Cowher was dressed smartly in a suit and tie, which he rarely wore for media sessions thereafter, and "was a little arrogant," by his own account some years later. But Cowher was also excited to coach his hometown team.

"When I had the opportunity to follow Chuck Noll, I knew I was coming to a team that knew how to work, how to prepare, and how to win," Cowher said later on. "But you don't even try to compare yourself to a man like Chuck Noll, and I haven't even come close to doing the things that he did. And no one will. He was one of a kind. So you don't even put yourself in that shadow. . . . I was very fortunate to be in that situation."

Gundy and other Steelers faithful were thrilled as well. Sure, there was some trepidation, but after more than a decade without a Super Bowl appearance, the Steelers Nation was ready for a new beginning—and the Cowher Era began for Steelers fans everywhere.

"I always liked Cowher," Gundy said. "I remember when he was a linebacker and special-teams guy with the Cleveland Browns and Philadelphia Eagles; and he coached with the Browns and the Kansas City Chiefs. Chuck Noll was a great coach, who had some great teams in the '70s, but I thought he was maybe getting a little complacent or predictable.

"I thought the same thing about Tom Landry with the Dallas Cowboys and Don Shula with the Miami Dolphins. Maybe none of them had the players that they had before, but they're responsible for that, too."

Gundy pointed out that the great Steelers teams in the 1970s weren't too fancy, either—running the ball with Harris and Rocky Bleier and with Bradshaw throwing downfield to Lynn Swann and John Stallworth—but through free agency in the NFL, the salary cap, expansion, and other changes, it was much more difficult to keep a good team together. Other than a solid core of players, teams had to let guys go. Every team was affected by these developments, and the Steelers were no different.

It's likely that they would not have been able to sustain a similar level of excellence with the same group of players from those four Super Bowl teams during this era. But Gundy and his newfound friends were excited to see what Cowher could do. That's why Gundy began a Steelers fan club in the Cape Coral-Fort Myers, Florida area. They met every Sunday at the same club to cheer the Steelers to victory after victory.

Gundy said that the group would meet there at noon each week, have lunch and talk sports. It was a football fan's dream day—TVs everywhere with a game on each one, good food, and spirited conversation. Gundy's Steelers club quickly became dominant in the club. At one point, Gundy noted, the group grew to some 100 members strong. It thrived almost immediately and took over an entire section at the Players Sports Emporium.

If a fan wasn't a big drinker or didn't like to eat much, it wouldn't cost much for him to be a member. Gundy recalled that each person paid a couple dollars to a kitty. Part of the money went to the bar for letting them watch the games there, and the rest went to prizes to raffle off during the day.

"You could get a cap or a shirt for $10-12 or so, and a pitcher of beer was a lot cheaper back then, too," Gundy said. "So it didn't cost us much, and everybody had a good time. It helped if the Steelers won, of course, but we had a real good time no matter what. We were all big Steelers fans."

The Steelers fan club in Fort Myers-Cape Coral ran strong for "quite a few good years, that I can remember," Gundy said. "I lasted (four) until Cowher's first Super Bowl trip after the 1995 season." The fan club was born in 1992, the same day that the Cowher Era began with the Steelers, when the team opened with the Houston Oilers at the Astrodome.

The Steelers trailed in the early going, 14-0, to their AFC Central Division rival. The Oilers were also favored to win the division that season, since the Steelers appeared to be in a state of flux with a new coach on the sideline for the first time since 1968, and a new starting quarterback in Neil O'Donnell. He beat out incumbent Bubby Brister in an extremely close preseason battle. Sure, there were several

Rookie Steelers coach Bill Cowher speaks with quarterback Neil O'Donnell on the sideline in 1992.

holdovers on a solid defensive unit, but that group was relatively unproven as well.

So Cowher, the second youngest NFL head coach—ironically, the same age as Houston quarterback Warren Moon—would have to pull out all the stops for the Steelers to begin the Cowher Era with a victory in the Astrodome, where they had not won a regular-season game since 1988.

"You have to do it your way, and you have to be yourself," Cowher said. "There's no blueprint to being a head coach . . . . You have to be yourself, because every situation is different. All you can do is respect your coaches and players, and you'll have more good times than bad."

That became more evident as the Oilers raced to an early 14-0 lead when linebacker Johnny Meads returned a fumble 15 yards for a touchdown after nearly 12 scoreless minutes. About three minutes later, Houston scored again on an 11-yard touchdown pass from Moon to Ernest Givins with 5:06 remaining in the first quarter. It was just a two-play, 26-yard, 53-second drive for the big-play Oilers early in the game.

The Steelers offense, however, just couldn't get going with O'Donnell's passing and power running from Barry Foster. Their ensuing drive started at the 20, and O'Donnell directed it past midfield before it hit a snag. On third down, O'Donnell was sacked for a double-figure loss in yardage to take the Steelers out of Gary Anderson's field-goal range. So punter Mark Royals took the field on fourth-and-long.

The 6-foot-5, 225-pound Royals wasn't too athletic, but Cowher knew he was adept at pinning opponents close to their own goal line. He knocked one-fourth of his punts inside the 20-yard line, and 15 percent of the time they nailed the opposition inside the 10. Cowher used Royals as a weapon that way, not taking too many chances on missed long field goals, so his defense would have an opportunity to make something happen. That was Cowher's background as a defensive coach coming out. He was Marty Schottenheimer's defensive coordinator for the Kansas City Chiefs, and also coached for him with the Cleveland Browns. When Cowher resigned after the 2006 season, Schottenheimer said the young coach was so relentless in pursuing the defensive coordinator position in 1989 that he eventually had to hire him. Cowher thanked Schottenheimer for giving him a start in coaching and the Rooneys for taking a chance on hiring him as the head coach for the Steelers. He rarely reflected during his time with the club, but that's what his final news conference was all about.

"We've had some disappointments, the AFC championship games when we got so close, but I can honestly say that was the fuel that brought me back and made me appreciate things."

The Steelers players certainly appreciated what Cowher did for them. He was a players' coach, to be sure, and he was extremely emotional; but he brought out the best in his players. All-Pro guard Alan Faneca gave credit to Cowher for leading the Steelers wherever they went. Inside linebacker Larry Foote praised him as well.

"What I'll miss most is his passion," Foote said. "Certain coaches and certain people, when they give speeches, you're not really listening to them. But the one thing I give him a lot of credit for is the tight ship that he ran. You see teams that have disappointing seasons, and they fall apart, but Coach Cowher keeps a tight ship. Players are not fighting with each other, not going off on coaches in the media. That's a credit to him, and it's why we respect him the most."

The Steelers' 2-4 mark in AFC title games under Cowher was his most substandard work through 15 seasons, but there were far more positive aspects to his tenure that began on that day at the Astrodome.

Cowher had fond memories from that initial matchup against the Oilers as well, but he likely never imagined what he would accomplish in 15 seasons with the Steelers. Cowher opened his coaching career with six straight playoff appearances, tying an NFL record, and led the Steelers to the postseason 10 times. They played in six AFC title games, including five at home, and went to Super Bowls after the 1995 and 2005 seasons with a victory—the franchise's fifth overall—in Super Bowl XL February 6, 2006, after a stunning 4-0 playoff run as the sixth seed on the road.

Cowher ended his coaching career—at least for the time being—with a 161-99-1 record, including an 8-8 mark in his final season (2006) and 12-9 record in the postseason. Cowher ranked third in winning percentage among NFL coaches in the 15 years since he took over in 1992.

The Oilers should have figured out pretty early that their matchup against the Cowher-led Steelers would be much different than the ones the team played the previous 23 seasons with Noll at the helm. Instead of punting the ball to pin the Oilers deep in their own territory like he had done many times before, Royals took the snap and tossed the ball downfield. The play resulted in a 44-yard pass to backup running back Warren Williams. The play keyed the Steelers' first score, a one-yard touchdown run by Foster. Cowher also called for several end-around plays, including one by speedy wideout Dwight Stone that went for 18 yards on a third-down play. That helped run out the clock to seal the Steelers' stunning 29-24 win at Houston.

"[I recall] the fake punt from the first game," Cowher said. "John Guy was our special-teams coach, and I told him I wanted to run the fake punt when we were inside the 50 because [Houston coach Jack Pardee] always rushed the punter. So there was a third-down-and-seven play.

"Neil got sacked for about 15 yards, so we were on our own 45 and I was wondering what happened. . . . Then I looked over at John and asked him if he was running the fake punt. He said I told him to do it, but if I had had time to think about it, like now, I probably wouldn't have run it."

That fake punt, though, was something that Cowher had been waiting to use for a while. They practiced it during training camp and the preseason and honed it during the week before the regular-season opener in Houston.

"We took a gamble because they were in a heavy-rush format," Cowher said. "It worked this time. (But) we had to take chances to come out of here victorious. You can't play conservatively on the road and expect to win all the time. I think we came in and stole one (to) beat the Oilers in Houston."

O'Donnell completed 14 of 23 passes for 223 yards with two touchdowns, including the game-winning nine-yard scoring toss to backup tight end Adrian Cooper with about eight minutes remaining. More importantly, though, he did not throw an interception. Moon, in possibly the poorest performance in his illustrious career in Canada and the NFL, was 29-for-45 for 330 yards. But he was picked off five times by the Steelers.

Cornerbacks Rod Woodson, hobbled by a leg injury, and Larry Griffin had two interceptions each. Safety Darren Perry also picked off Moon, who now had thrown 15 interceptions in the past four games against the Steelers. They had picked him off five times in the previous season's game at Three Rivers Stadium in Pittsburgh as well.

"Our defense gave us so many opportunities, and we had come up with only three points," O'Donnell said. "We needed to make more of our opportunities. We were lucky to get off some big plays because of their pass rush, but we were able to take advantage of some of their overplay."

And Houston veteran coach Jack Pardee and his staff were unprepared to counteract the Steelers' calls.

"There is no one phase of the game that cost us the game," Pardee said. "There were just a number of things that happened. (Moon) still had almost 400 passing yards. You just have to put (more) points on the board."

Moon was intercepted on just his fourth pass, with Woodson returning the ball 16 yards to the Houston 37, but the Steelers failed to capitalize. However, interceptions by Perry and Griffin led to a 30-yard field goal by Gary Anderson 1:51 into the second quarter. A few minutes later, O'Donnell threw a 20-yard touchdown pass to Jeff Graham to trim Houston's lead to 17-16.

Woodson returned his second interception 57 yards, and Foster ran 19 on the next play to set up the touchdown catch by Cooper that basically won the game. He had replaced injured starter Eric Green.

Moon tried to rally the Oilers. He hit wideout Haywood Jeffries with a 57-yard pass and Leonard Harris for five yards to the Pittsburgh 14; but Griffin picked off Moon's next pass and returned it 27 yards with 2:09 left. Moon's two touchdown passes were for 11 and eight yards to Ernest Givins, but the five interceptions prompted boos from the more than 60,000 Houston fans in attendance. The five picks tied Moon's career high, which also came against the Steelers the previous season in Pittsburgh.

"I deserved it," Moon said. "Hey, we lost this game because I didn't make the plays. Our fans have been let down for a long time. We came into this game as one of the Super Bowl favorites, and then we play like this. I'm still trying to recap what happened. It's still a blur to me. I can't believe the way we lost the game, and I can't believe the way I played at times."

Rather than use the Steelers defense as an excuse, Moon chose to examine his own poor judgment and erratic throws.

"I just stunk, especially when I needed to be at my best," Moon said. "I had a chance to make some plays when we needed them and didn't do it. I'm just thankful this happened in the first game and that we have 15 more left. You can be sure this isn't indicative of how I will play the rest of the season.

"So, I'm not going to let this get me down. I know I'm going to get a lot of criticism, and I deserve it. It comes with the position. But I'm going to try to keep a positive attitude and try to help my teammates keep a positive attitude as well this week in practice."

On the other side of the ball, the Steelers offense was solid. Along with O'Donnell's passing numbers, Foster had 26 carries for 107 yards and one score, while Anderson kicked three field goals. But it was Cowher's boldness that separated the Steelers from the Oilers that day.

The game marked a new beginning for the Steelers franchise, and fans like Gundy and his fellow members of the Fort Myers–Cape Coral Steelers club were extremely happy about that.

14

TAKING CHARGE

O'Donnell Leads Comeback
Soldier Field
Chicago, Illinois
November 5, 1995

SHAWN KENNEDY AND JEFF HERTZOG were thrown together as roommates at tiny Milligan College nestled in the foothills of the Great Smokey Mountains in the Northeast corner of Tennessee, near Johnson City, and about a 60-minute drive across the border to Asheville, North Carolina.

Kennedy and Hertzog believed they had little in common, at first, but eventually found common interests in music and a certain NFL team. However, while their tastes in music might have evolved over the years, the duo's bond with the Pittsburgh Steelers has strengthened, leading them through many good times and helping to develop a friendship that has been maintained to this day.

While Kennedy is a Pittsburgh native, Hertzog was born and raised in Virginia. Kennedy first attended Perry High School in Pittsburgh's City League before transferring to Thomas Jefferson as a sophomore after his family moved to the South Hills. "I've been a Steelers fan since I was born," Kennedy proclaimed.

Hertzog, however, didn't let his proximity to the city alter his football interests. He was indoctrinated into loving the Steelers at an early age since his parents and other family members are from the

143

Pittsburgh area, and he considers it to be a second home. "We grew up loving the Steelers," Hertzog said.

The two wore their Steelers gear with pride while in college and certainly when watching games at local watering holes. But they were in the minority, by far, as the Tennessee Titans ruled NFL followers in that area and college football fans mostly "wore obnoxious orange," Kennedy noted, for the Tennessee Volunteers. Their fans are rabid, but Kennedy and Hertzog stayed the course and always secured a small corner at a local club where a handful of Steelers fans could watch the weekly games.

Inexplicably, that number grew to 15-20 Steelers fans on a regular basis, so a larger area in the bar was needed. As the Steelers fortunes improved and were well on their way to a spectacular 15-1 regular season in 2004, their faithful fans in Tennessee grew exponentially to about 100. Tables were reserved, and the Titans were pushed off the main screen. Even the local Volunteers following had difficulty competing with their numbers.

"We started to take over the place," Hertzog said. "They did a lot for us, but it was good for the bar, too, because we spent a lot of money there."

As the Steelers made their run to the playoffs in 2005 and an eventual Super Bowl XL championship, they played archrival Cincinnati at Heinz Field. The game was exciting from start to finish, and the Bengals eventually pulled out a 38-31 victory to push the Steelers' losing streak to three games and their record to 7-5. They looked like anything but a Super Bowl team to that point, but they were getting healthier. Quarterback Ben Roethlisberger was rounding back into shape after a knee injury, and the defense was gaining strength. So was their following in Tennessee.

"We had people everywhere for that Cincinnati game," Kennedy said. "There were Steelers fans blocking the aisles, and that made it tough for the bar's staff to move around."

One bar manager, who Kennedy said happened to be a Bengals fan, voiced his displeasure. It seems he didn't value the heavy Steelers presence, despite all the money the bar made off them. According to Kennedy, the manager basically said: "You damn

The Steel City Mafia "bosses" Shawn Kennedy, Jeff Hertzog, and Jeremy Kinnard pose with former Steelers linebacker Greg Lloyd.

Steelers fans, you're everywhere. You think you run this place? You're like the mafia."

Instead of being insulted, Kennedy and Hertzog liked the idea. Actually, they embraced it and began calling themselves the Steelers Mafia, because they enjoyed being part of the Steelers' close-knit family of fans. Then they started to have some fun with the concept. Hertzog started a MySpace page, an internet forum to meet people and keep in touch with them, and it really took off. Those who became involved didn't realize that the Steelers Mafia was just a local football fan club in Tennessee. But with the internet, worldwide access was possible.

Duane Smyth was born in West Berlin, Germany, where his father was stationed in the Air Force. Smyth and his family moved to Nebraska for a while and then to the Denver area. Yet Smith's mother was born and raised in Butler, Pennsylvania, north of Pittsburgh. The family returned to that area and has remained ever since.

"My mom was a Broncos fan growing up, until I was 16, but I started to get more involved as a Steelers fan," Smyth said. "She finally came around and was a true Steelers fan by the time she passed away in 1999."

Smyth gives the group a presence in the Pittsburgh area. He met Hertzog at an event near the city, kept in contact primarily through MySpace, and met the rest during another event in Monroeville. Smyth added that he has handed out quite a few business cards since then, and his "family" is growing along with the others.

Jeremy Kinnard was born in Colorado and currently resides in Marietta, Ohio, less than three hours from Pittsburgh, but he's been a Steelers fan since 1990 and has become heavily involved. It goes like this: Kinnard would say, "Family, Steelers, food and air, something like that." Kinnard uses MySpace on a regular basis, so he became acquainted with Kennedy and Hertzog through the internet, and they all quickly became friends.

Kinnard eventually jumped in a car and drove to Tennessee to meet his fellow Steelers fans on one fateful Saturday afternoon, and the Steel City Mafia was born "to unite Steelers fans worldwide in the common interest of developing fan recognition, fan benefits and a positive fan presence in the community," according to the organization's mission statement. The Steel City Mafia Web site was started, and fan clubs were organized. Some were already in place, while others were created. Access to the internet has given new meaning to the term "information superhighway," and the Pittsburgh Steelers Nation has taken advantage of it.

The team's followers reach far and wide and not just in the United States, but overseas as well. Just browsing the internet provides Steelers fans with information about their favorite NFL team more quickly and effortlessly than saying Troy Polamalu. Just conduct a search for Pittsburgh Steelers Nation, for example, and you'll get more than 1.3 million results.

"It's amazing, when you think about it," Hertzog said. "We knew the Steelers had a strong following around the world, but this has really taken off for us.

"We'd love to have an event at every Steelers game each season, and we definitely want to do them with clubs in the cities for every road game. The home games, there's a lot going on, so it's more difficult to do something there. But we're trying. We're reaching out to all the cities."

Steelers clubs range from Florida to California, Hawaii to England and even to Mars—Pennsylvania, of course—but you get the idea. Since its inception in July 2006 and in less than one year, the Steel City Mafia has grown immensely. There were 4,659 registered members across all 50 states, in Washington, D.C., and in Europe in an early 2007 count. Sure, the SCM understands implications with the term mafia might not be favorable, but the organization's "bosses" believe that others should realize that the SCM refers to the positive family aspects found only among Steelers fans.

But be forewarned, the Web site suggests that Steelers fans don't condone or encourage any criminal behavior or illegal activity, unless it takes place in the form of a bone-crunching hit on the football field, of course, and the fans are everywhere. So they'll soon take over your town, and you can try to do anything you want to them. However, they are strong, and they are here to stay.

"We want to spread the word to as many people as possible about the Steelers," Kennedy said. "We haven't been organized for very long, but we're doing pretty well. Someday, we want to be the largest fan club in the world."

Access the SCM Web site at www.steelcitymafia.com to learn about becoming a family member. A portion of all membership dues are donated to Jerome Bettis' "The Bus Stops Here Foundation." Official events occur on NFL football weekends during the season and, of course, are centered around a Steelers game.

Current and former players have even gotten involved as "Made" members in the Steel City Mafia. The group includes Dermontti Dawson, Kevin Greene, Rocky Bleier, Jeff Hartings, Greg Lloyd, Jason Gildon, Andy Russell, Santonio Holmes, Willie Parker, Myron Cope, Ryan Clark, Bryant McFadden, James Harrison, Larry Foote, Franco Harris, and Hines Ward. There are others, and more are expected to join the Family soon.

Steelers fans didn't need to be organized to travel to Chicago for a matchup against the Bears in 1995. They attended the game because it was critical in the club's attempt to finally return to the

Super Bowl. The Steelers had lost in the AFC championship game after the previous season, only the third under new coach Bill Cowher, and they wanted another shot at the big game. But the Steelers were 3-3 when the AFC Central took a week off and lost the next game at home to Cincinnati after that. They then beat Jacksonville at Three Rivers Stadium to move to 4-4 and couldn't afford another setback against the Bears. The team appeared to be back on track after its roller-coaster start, but this week wouldn't be easy, even with a legion of Steelers fans certain to be in attendance.

The Bears were a good team under then-coach Dave Wannstedt with a 6-2 record and a first-place perch in the NFC Central Division, but that was only the tip of the iceberg. The Steelers franchise was 0-for-forever in Chicago or 0-for-11 to be more precise. They first played in the Windy City in 1936 and lost, last played there in 1992 and lost and were a solid 0-for-9 in between. That was one miserable losing streak with no wins in nearly a six-decade span. Even during the Steelers' first 40 woeful years in existence, they didn't compile such a pitiful stretch. They were 0-11-1 in Los Angeles against the Rams, but beat the Raiders four times there.

"No visit to Chicago has been a good one for the Steelers," Cowher said during his weekly pregame press conference. "The law of averages should be going our way."

This game could be the turning point for the season. Had the Steelers lost, they would have dropped below .500 and many changes would be in order. A victory, however, could propel them on a winning streak that would secure a playoff berth and lead to another shot at the Super Bowl.

The Steelers didn't appear to be ready to snap the losing skid in Chicago any time soon despite an early drive deep into Bears' territory. However, Steelers running back Erric Pegram fumbled on the 11 to keep his club off the scoreboard, and Chicago place-kicker Kevin Butler booted a 40-yard field goal for a 3-0 first-quarter advantage. The Steelers opened up their offense in the second quarter, as Pegram scored twice and Norm Johnson added a 40-yard field goal to give them a 17-10 halftime lead.

Pegram's one-yard plunge 5:18 into the second quarter gave the Steelers a 7-3 advantage, but Chicago regained it on quarterback Erik Kramer's six-yard scoring pass to Curtis Conway. Johnson kicked his field goal less than three minutes before halftime, but the Steelers got the ball back and scored again with 1:39 remaining on quarterback Neil O'Donnell's seven-yard touchdown pass to Pegram. It was his first NFL TD catch.

The Bears owned the third quarter with two touchdowns, while Johnson's 46-yard field goal was the only Steelers' score. Pegram's second fumble came at the Steelers' 32-yard line and later led to a Chicago score. Kramer connected with fullback Tony Carter from 12 yards out to tie the score at 17-17. He also hooked up with tight end Ryan Wetnight for a 14-yard scoring pass, and the Bears led 24-20 after three. Chicago padded its lead with Butler's 27-yard field goal just 10 seconds into the final quarter, but it was crucial for the Steelers to keep the Bears out of the end zone.

Pegram, who rushed for 61 yards on 24 carries, made amends for his earlier miscues with a six-yard touchdown run in the fourth quarter that tied the score at 27-27. The Steelers decided to throw from their own end zone during the ensuing possession, but O'Donnell was picked off. Linebacker Barry Minter ran the interception in from the 2 for the go-ahead touchdown, and the lead changed hands for the third time. The teams traded punts, but the Steelers methodically drove into Bears territory with the game in the balance and time running out on a chance to tie the score for the fourth time to force an overtime period. Two runs from the Chicago 10 went for minus-1 yards for the Steelers, so O'Donnell dropped back to pass on third down.

Pegram was the key in this drive that lasted more than eight minutes. He already had three touchdowns in the game, and the former Atlanta Falcons discard had scored just five times in four previous NFL seasons. Pegram was a featured back for the Steelers against Chicago because bulldozer Bam Morris was out with a back injury. The powerful Morris and slashing Pegram usually gave the Steelers a solid one-two punch in their running game, but not on this day. So Pegram carried the load for the Steelers and had several big runs to get the club into scoring range.

"What you need to know about (Pegram) is that he goes out and produces," Steelers wideout Andre Hastings said. "That's all he does. He produces."

At 5-foot-10 and 195 pounds, Pegram wasn't the biggest NFL back, but he was tough and was a solid replacement for Foster. And he usually didn't fumble so much, either. He had a chance to make up for his fumbles during the waning moments in regulation.

"Everyone was telling me not to worry about [the fumbles], but I was taking it personally," Pegram said. "I had to redeem myself. . . ."

O'Donnell needed to stick the ball into the end zone on this opportunity and would have taken third and even fourth down to try, but he fired to wideout Ernie Mills into the end zone on third down to get the Steelers within one, 34-33, with Johnson's extra point set to tie the score again. But O'Donnell didn't want to take the easy way out. He was hot, capping what would be a 34-for-52 passing day for 341 yards—his fourth career 300-plus-yard passing performance—and two scores to set a Steelers single-game completion record, and wanted to go for two points to win the game right then. Wideout Yancey Thigpen wanted to eschew overtime as well, but Cowher decided to go with Johnson's conversion kick to tie the score.

"O'Donnell threw that touchdown to Mills, and that was a big play," said Norm Vargo, a Steelers beat writer for the *McKeesport Daily News*. "We were standing on the sideline near that end zone when that happened, and the Bears crowd just went silent. All the Steelers fans went wild."

Reportedly, the Steelers would have used rookie Kordell Stewart, known as "Slash" for his versatility as a quarterback/running back/wide receiver that season, split out wide as a decoy. And O'Donnell, inconceivably, would run it in on a quarterback draw. Not known for his blazing speed—or any at all, for that matter—it seemed to be a good call on Cowher's part.

In any event, Johnson kicked the extra point with 1:06 remaining in regulation to send the game into overtime. During the OT period, the Steelers defense came up big by forcing a punt. And

Quarterback Neil O'Donnell led the Steelers to the Super Bowl in 1995.

when they got the ball back, Pegram again would be the key with five carries and one catch in the drive. O'Donnell also connected with Mills for an 11-yard hookup on a third-and-11 play. Pegram's reception changed field position for the Steelers, as he took a screen pass and raced 14 yards into Chicago territory. And to improve the club's field position on third-and-2 from the Bears 24, he squeezed through the line for a first down. Johnson eventually kicked a 24-yard field goal 8:19 into overtime to give the Steelers a stunning 37-34 victory.

"I think they were honoring some former player that day—something big was going on for the Bears—but they couldn't get it done," Vargo said. "The Steelers came back and won that game thanks to O'Donnell.

"He had a great day. There's no question the Steelers turned it around after that, showing that they were back that year after a tough start. That win on the road really got them going again."

The Steelers won another big game at Cincinnati two weeks later for their fourth straight victory and had four more wins in a row before a loss at Green Bay to finish at 11–5. The Steelers already clinched the AFC Central Division title, so the Packers game didn't matter. The club won an AFC divisional playoff against Buffalo, 40–21 at Three Rivers Stadium, and then beat the Indianapolis Colts, 20–16, in an exciting AFC title game at home.

The Super Bowl was a lot less thrilling for the Steelers. They got behind early and lost 27–17 to the Dallas Cowboys, as O'Donnell threw three interceptions and couldn't bring the club back from its deficit.

But at least the Steelers finally returned to the Super Bowl, and they never would have gotten there if O'Donnell didn't take charge in a midseason game at Chicago.

15

REDEMPTION

AFC Championship Game
Three Rivers Stadium
Pittsburgh, Pennsylvania
January 14, 1996

THE ULTIMATE WEDDING PRESENT for some couples might be a new home, a honeymoon cruise, a trip to a spa, or even a romantic balloon ride. But Kathy Lebeda found the perfect gift for her new husband, Bob, when she purchased season tickets to the Pittsburgh Steelers in 1973. The up-and-coming Steelers were fresh from a stunning playoff win against the hated Oakland Raiders and an unexpected appearance in the AFC championship game the previous season. Kathy believed it was a good idea to get on board as the team steadily improved.

"Season tickets were a lot cheaper back then, right after Three Rivers Stadium opened, and not tough to get because the Steelers weren't doing too well up to that point," Kathy recalled. "But I've been a football fan since I was a little kid, and Bob definitely was a big fan. So, I thought season tickets were a good idea.

"We had seats in the upper level in the end zone. I loved those seats. It was great to watch games from that vantage point."

Kathy, a self-described tomboy in her youth, used to go to Steelers games when they played at Pitt Stadium in the 1960s. When she met Bob, the two football fans hit it off almost immediately. Watching

Steelers games became part of their dating experience during football season. The two attended games together until Bob's job forced a move from Pittsburgh to California in 1982. They relocated to Oceanside, about 20 miles north of San Diego, and the Lebedas have been in the area now for nearly 25 years.

"We were going to split (Chargers) tickets with another couple when we first moved out here, but the first time we went to a Chargers game they scored and nobody cheered," Kathy said. "It was amazing. And you know how intense the Steelers fans are. They scream and carry on.

"So that was very strange for us out here. It's gotten a lot better since the Chargers have improved, but the fans just aren't the same out here as Steelers fans. We don't get to see the Steelers play too often out here and never live, but at least we get to see them occasionally on TV."

Thankfully for them, the Lebedas weren't in the Pittsburgh area during the late 1980s, when the Steelers hit their lowest period under coach Chuck Noll. On the other hand, they also missed the club's return to glory after Bill Cowher took over as the head coach in 1992. The Steelers were the AFC's top seed with an 11-5 record that season, but they lost a home game to the Buffalo Bills in the playoffs. They qualified for the playoffs again the next year with a 9-7 mark, but lost a first-round playoff game at Kansas City. In 1994, however, the Steelers were a dominant 12-4 with a 10-1 streak going into the regular-season finale at San Diego.

Without a sense of urgency to win that game, it's not surprising the Steelers lost, 37-34. They still had home-field advantage for the playoffs and pounded Cleveland 29-9 in the divisional round to earn another shot at San Diego. This time, though, the Steelers faced the Chargers at Heinz Field in the AFC title game. Despite being an overwhelming favorite and taking a 13-3 lead midway through the third quarter, the Steelers allowed two long touchdown passes by San Diego quarterback Stan Humphries and lost, 17-13.

"I basically guaranteed a victory," Bob said. "There were wagers going left and right, and my office was draped in black and gold. Boy, did I eat a lot of crow after that loss. For a week after that, they

Kathy and Bob Lebeda brought the Terrible Towel to sunny California.

decorated my office in Chargers colors. I just didn't think [the Chargers] could go in there and beat the Steelers. But you need a lot of luck, as well as being good, and the Chargers had a lot going for them on that day."

Bob and Kathy admitted that they cheer for the Chargers, as long as they're playing a team other than the Steelers. But deep down inside, they will always be big Black and Gold fans. But it's not easy to go at it alone in enemy territory.

"I really took a ribbing for losing to the Chargers in 1994," Kathy said. "I thought they were going to win for sure, so I went around telling everybody at work that there was no way the Chargers were going to win. . . . I got hassled a lot about that, but it was OK."

That's because the Steelers made another late-season run into the playoffs in 1995 as well. After the debacle in the 1994 AFC championship game, the Steelers basically devoted the ensuing season to redeeming that loss to the Chargers. The theme was "three more yards," because the Steelers had been stopped on the 3-yard line the year before. The team didn't bounce back too quickly, however, opening the '95 season with a 3-4 record. The Steelers got back on track with a crucial 24-7 win against Jacksonville at home and a 37-34 overtime victory at Chicago. On a roll, the team won eight straight to secure home-field advantage in the playoffs and an 11-5 regular-season record.

Kansas City earned the top seed with a 13-3 record and a first-round bye, but the Chiefs dropped a 10-7 decision to the Indianapolis Colts. The Steelers pounded the Bills in their playoff opener, 40-21, at home. That win earned the Steelers a spot in the AFC title game for the second straight season at home and a meeting with the Colts. Quarterback Jim Harbaugh led the upstart Colts as they beat the Chargers in the wild-card round and then edged the Chiefs to get a shot at the Steelers.

"We watched the [Indianapolis-Pittsburgh game] with just Steelers fans at our house," said Bob. "We had Terrible Towels on the TV and everything. We really went all out for that game."

Since Terrible Towels and other Steelers paraphernalia weren't readily available in the San Diego area, the Lebedas had to rely on friends and relatives in the Pittsburgh area for fan support. Kathy noted that her niece, Donna Olbrich, and her family sent all the Steelers clippings from the Pittsburgh newspapers, as well as T-shirts, jerseys, and even some Terrible Towels. Everything was in place for a win.

"Neither team did much on offense in the early going," Bob recalled. "But the Steelers played well enough on offense and were great on defense to build an early lead and keep it."

The highly favored Steelers pulled out a 10-7 halftime lead thanks to a late 5-yard touchdown pass from Neil O'Donnell to rookie Kordell Stewart. The touchdown created some controversy, as instant replay showed that Stewart had stepped out of bounds in the back of the end zone and then came back in to make the catch. He could have been called for illegal touching, but it was difficult to determine if Stewart had stepped out during his route or if he was pushed out. None of that mattered, because there was no flag and the touchdown stood.

O'Donnell did a nice job keeping the play alive long enough to get the ball to Stewart for the score. He might not have made that play earlier in his career, but O'Donnell had matured thanks to a great season—among the best single-season marks for a Steelers quarterback, completing 59.1 percent of his passes for 2,970 yards and 17 touchdowns—and his strong play continued in the playoffs.

Erric Pegram and Bam Morris also gave the Steelers a solid one-two combination at running back that season, with the speedy Pegram slashing for 813 yards and five touchdowns, while Morris ran for 559 yards and nine scores. Yancey Thigpen led the Steelers' wideout corps with 85 catches for 1,307 yards and five touchdowns. Andre Hastings, Ernie Mills, and rookie Charles Johnson provided depth at the receiver position.

The Colts weren't without a few offensive weapons of their own, including "Captain Comeback" in quarterback Jim Harbaugh. The Steelers' 13-9 advantage held up until 6:14 into the fourth quarter, when Harbaugh connected on a 47-yard touchdown pass to Floyd Turner. Cue the eerie feeling of déjà vu for Steelers fans.

"Don't remind me," Bob said. "All we could think of was the previous year's collapse against the Chargers. It really was unbelievable that it was happening again. But there was still a lot of time left."

The Steelers couldn't do anything on their next drive, however, and the Colts got the ball back with designs on running out the clock. The Steelers' previous Super Bowl runs were fueled by an aggressive, hard-nosed defensive unit, and this club was no different. It was the defense that had let the Steelers down the previous season by allowing several big plays during the fourth quarter against the Chargers. If they were going to reach Super Bowl XXX—their first appearance on the game's biggest stage in 16 years—the defense would need to make a difference again, but in a positive way this time.

A third-year pro, Steelers cornerback Willie Williams had enjoyed a spectacular season, picking off seven passes from the defensive backfield and even returning one interception for a touchdown. But no regular-season play was as big as the one he turned in during the

AFC title game against the Colts that season. On a third-and-one play during that key Indy drive, Williams bolted into the backfield from his secondary spot and tackled Colts fullback Lamont Warren from behind just as Warren was hitting his stride toward a gaping hole. Had Williams not made this incredible tackle, the Colts most assuredly would have been deep in Steelers territory and could have sealed the win. Indy might have gotten a field goal and certainly could have run out the clock.

"We were well-coached on that play, and I was looking for Warren to get the ball," Williams said. "I really didn't do anything special on the play, though. I had a clear shot at him, and I just blew into the backfield and knocked him down. . . . We had the right defense called, and I just did my job."

The Steelers got the ball back with an opportunity to finish off a game-winning drive, something they failed to do the previous year. O'Donnell and his talented wideouts strung together some plays, but the drive nearly stalled at midfield. Pittsburgh was faced with a fourth-and-three, and O'Donnell hit Hastings for a nine-yard gain to the 38. On the ensuing play, he fired downfield to Mills, who hauled in the long bomb at the 1-yard line. Two plays later Morris scored, and Johnson's extra point gave the Steelers a 20-16 advantage with just 1:34 remaining.

Starting at Indy's 16-yard line, Harbaugh led a furious Colts drive to the Steelers 29 that included a huge fourth-down conversion. With time for just one play, Harbaugh needed Divine Intervention. He launched a "Hail Mary" pass into the end zone that was tipped several times before being deflected to the ground by Steelers cornerback Randy Fuller.

"When that ball went up, we all thought we had a shot at it," Williams said. "We didn't know what happened right away, but it just couldn't be caught by the Colts. After losing to San Diego the previous year at home, we needed to beat the Colts. We needed to win at home to get to the Super Bowl."

Network television commentator Phil Simms screamed that Indianapolis' Aaron Bailey had caught Harbaugh's Hail Mary, but veteran play-by-play man Dick Enberg quickly corrected him. There would be no collapse this year—the Steelers were victorious and headed to the franchise's fifth Super Bowl.

"That last play," Bob said, "when the ball hit the ground and was incomplete, it was just a great feeling. We couldn't believe it. They finally made it back to the Super Bowl, and we were so excited. It took a long time for the Steelers to get there, but it was a great feeling."

The Steelers would go on to lose Super Bowl XXX to the Cowboys. But they had cleared an important hurdle on the way. A second straight loss in the AFC title game—at home, nonetheless—would have been devastating. Concerning the Super Bowl defeat . . . well, making up for that would have to come at another time.

16

A COMING OF AGE

Roethlisberger's First NFL Start
Dolphin Stadium
Davie, Florida
September 26, 2004

TONY GRECO TRIES NOT TO MISS Pittsburgh Steelers games when they're on television. But when he got an opportunity to attend a Steelers game in Florida with some relatives, he of course jumped at the chance. Had he known what was coming, he might have just said "No thanks" ahead of time and saved himself the trouble. Little did Greco know, but Mother Nature had her own plans for that particular Sunday, and it would not be kind to those hoping to play football.

As Greco and his relatives, Tom Fullard and Scott Strager, planned for their trip to the Miami area to meet up with siblings Dallas and Brea Strager, Hurricane Jeanne was gaining strength. Fullard, Scott, and his family made it to Florida, despite heavy rain, but Greco never got on the plane.

"I was working a high school football game between Moon and Ambridge, so I didn't plan on leaving until Saturday morning," Greco said. "I had my bags packed and everything, but with all the weather problems every flight from Pittsburgh to Florida was canceled. And I was stuck at home."

Greco had hoped that the game would be postponed so he could still make the trip, but only the start time changed, moving from 1 p.m. to 8:30 p.m.

Instead of getting on a plane for Florida, Greco went to Heinz Field to watch his University of Pittsburgh Panthers struggle to a win against Division I-AA Furman. And he was forced to watch the Steelers-Dolphins game on television Sunday night. Fullard and the Stragers had other problems.

"I thought this would be a great getaway for the end of the summer, but we really didn't know what we were getting into," Fullard said.

Fullard and the Stragers arrived Friday, two days before the game, and were set up by Brea Strager in the hotel where she worked. They enjoyed the weather through Friday night, blissfully unaware about what they would face over the weekend. The rain began sometime overnight, continued in the morning and steadily gained momentum.

Dallas lives in Boca Raton, about 20 miles north of Fort Lauderdale, and he supplemented his full-time job with part-time work for the Miami Dolphins. A self-described Steelers fan behind enemy lines, Dallas normally would be on the field all day, handling game-day operations, tunnel preparations, and introductions. But he wouldn't work this game like his girlfriend, Dolphins cheerleader Lauren Merola, also from the Pittsburgh area. Partying and good times were on the agenda with his relatives, but those plans changed about as quickly as the weather conditions.

"We were getting ready to go out for the day on Saturday," Fullard said. "Everybody said we would be OK, but practically the minute I got off the phone with Brea an evacuation notice was slid under my door at the hotel. Brea said the hotel would take care of us, but we were out of there."

The group went to Dallas' apartment in Boca Raton and hoped to avoid Hurricane Jeanne there. Dallas, in his eighth year in South Florida, had seen this situation before. He believed the storm would veer off and move away from the state, but the hurricane watch quickly turned to a warning and conditions became grave.

"We really weren't sure what to do, but I didn't have much food in my fridge and certainly not enough for all of us," Dallas said. "So

COURTESY OF TONY GRECO

Tony Greco (on right) and friends Brian Karavlan and Jodi Newman pose before a game.

the first thing we decided to do was make a food and beer run. But places were starting to close, due to the hurricane warning, and all we could find was a 7-Eleven that we basically emptied."

The group still didn't know the status of the game or when they could get home, because planes left the area immediately so they wouldn't get stuck there. So they killed time—and weathered the storm—in the new Hard Rock Casino in the area. And a good time was had by all.

When they awoke Sunday morning, they found out the game was postponed until later that night, but weather conditions did not improve much. It still rained steadily, but didn't stop them from heading to Dolphins Stadium to tailgate. Amazingly, Fullard and the Stragers weren't the only Steelers fans in attendance. They were there by the busload, "maybe 20 (busses)," Fullard said, and the group wanted to party with them.

"It was great," Dallas said. "We were all cheering for the Steelers, and it continued inside for the game. But the weather was horrendous. It was like a waterfall going down the steps of the stadium. The field looked like a mud pit, and I think the weather was getting worse with every play."

Several first-half downpours, caused by remnants from Hurricane Jeanne, left standing water in the baseball infield, which made footing especially treacherous there. The start of the second half was delayed so the grounds crew could apply additional bags of dirt.

"That was the worst weather I ever played in," Steelers wideout Hines Ward said, but that didn't stop him and his teammates from moving the ball. Still, neither quarterback could throw the football too efficiently.

"The weather in the first half was not conducive to doing anything," Steelers coach Bill Cowher said. "We couldn't even hold the ball. Both teams couldn't throw it. But that's the kind of football I love."

Cowher had to love his defense, too. It held the Dolphins to 169 total yards and bruised more than just their pride. A jarring tackle by Steelers free safety Chris Hope sent running back Lamar Gordon from the game with an injured left shoulder. It later was determined that Gordon had a dislocated shoulder and was ruled out for the season. Even before the heaviest rain, the Steelers forced three turnovers on Miami's first seven plays.

The Steelers got a 40-yard field goal from place-kicker Jeff Reed nearly seven minutes into the first quarter, as Steelers rookie quarterback Ben Roethlisberger hooked up with wide receiver Plaxico Burress for a 42-yard gain to set it up. Burress made a diving catch on the play, but there wasn't much more action in the first half.

Trailing 3-0 early in the second half, Miami coach Dave Wannstedt gambled by going for it on fourth-and-one at the Miami 47, but quarterback A.J. Feeley was stopped for no gain on a sneak. Six plays later, Reed hit a 51-yard field goal.

Miami's best drive covered 44 yards to set up a 34-yard Olindo Mare field goal 1:35 into the fourth quarter to make it 6-3. But Roethlisberger, who was intercepted on his first pass as a starter, kept battling back. Filling in for the injured Tommy Maddox, Roethlisberger mounted a Steelers drive midway through the fourth quarter that reached the 7-yard line, and the rookie looked for the end zone on the next play.

This situation is just what the Steelers hoped for when they selected Roethlisberger with the No. 11 pick in the first round of the 2004 NFL Draft. Sure, they planned for it to come a little later in his career, not as a rookie, but to coin a phrase from Cowher the situation "is what it is." The club earned the right to choose Roethlisberger that high in the draft after finishing 6-10 in 2003. They were 1-1 during this season, going into the third game at Miami, with a win in the opener and loss at Baltimore when Maddox was hurt. Roethlisberger played well, at times, but couldn't do enough to win the Baltimore game. He was 12-for-20 in his Steelers debut with two touchdown passes and two interceptions.

Still, the young quarterback showed a lot of promise in that game, despite a limited game plan, and displayed similar toughness and grittiness at Miami. Steelers followers everywhere, as well as Cowher and the coaching staff, quickly sensed that he was destined for greatness. Roethlisberger would be the team's franchise quarterback, one who could lead them back to the Super Bowl and finally secure that one for the thumb.

"We knew he had something," Ward said. "That's for sure."

But it didn't start out that way. All-Pro guard Alan Faneca wasn't too kind a few days earlier when asked his thoughts about having the rookie quarterback lead the Steelers that week against the Dolphins.

"How would you like to have a young kid go to work with you?" Faneca replied to the reporters. "It's not really exciting for us or something we're looking forward to right now."

Ken Whisenhunt, the Steelers' offensive coordinator, believed that Roethlisberger would play some as a rookie but not be a starter. He wanted the quarterback to be brought along slowly, like his mentor Joe Gibbs did with his young guys with the Washington Redskins.

"I'm more than willing to do whatever it is that Coach asks of me and what's best for the team, whether that's coming in and playing right now or learning behind Tommy for a little while," Roethlisberger said on draft day.

Maddox was quite popular with his teammates, and they didn't appreciate this brash kid coming in and taking charge. But there was something missing from the Steelers at that point. They just didn't know at the time that it was a quarterback like Roethlisberger. He would help them return to playing the type of football that the Steelers are noted for, a power running game featuring big plays on offense and a physical defense.

The Steelers needed something to unite them. The injury to Maddox could have divided the team, but it didn't. Hurricane Jeanne also helped, in a way. While the team was at its hotel the night before the game, the power went out. Players gathered together in the hallway, sitting under the emergency lighting while sharing stories.

"We just talked," cornerback Deshea Townsend said. "We got to know each other better. It's not important what was said, but it really made us closer as a team. Tighter. We needed something, I didn't know what, but we weren't winning. I guess that made a big difference."

And so did Roethlisberger. He was strong and cool under pressure—able to make things happen long after a play broke down. At 6-foot-5 and about 240 pounds, Roethlisberger couldn't be knocked down with one hit. And he couldn't be rattled. He wasn't fast, but he could move around quickly in the pocket and get outside when his protection broke down. And he made plays, many more than his predecessors at quarterback for the Steelers.

Sure, Kordell Stewart was fast and strong, and he could beat an opponent with his legs or his arm. He had a successful run with the Steelers, but he wasn't the answer. He couldn't get them past the AFC title game. Maddox set record passing numbers and made the Steelers offense more exciting than ever, but he threw as many interceptions as touchdowns—many of which were returned for opponents' scores—and he didn't win nearly enough.

Then, there's Roethlisberger, who had plenty of potential but still much to prove. The Steelers coaching staff watered down the playbook for the Miami game.

"We didn't want him thinking too much out there, worrying about a certain play or whatever," Whisenhunt said. "We just wanted him to hand the ball off, complete some passes when necessary and not turn the ball over over. The game plan was as simplistic as we could make it."

Hurricane Jeanne altered those plans even more.

"It was a crazy time down here, but that's what you have to deal with when you live in South Florida," Dallas Strager said. "I can't imagine what the Steelers were going through that weekend, but Ben looked all right. I think, being a new guy in the league, this was a perfect situation for him."

Fullard agreed with him and noted that the Steelers and their fans appeared to be recharged when Roethlisberger took over the offense.

"To me, it looked like Ben was a talented quarterback who they were going to have to keep in reserve," Fullard said. "They weren't going to stick him in there right away, but they had to. And it was just an explosion after that. The team just seemed to come together, and the fans loved it."

Dallas believed that Steelers fans were pulling for Roethlisberger from the outset. The Steelers faithful in attendance didn't even boo him when his first pass was intercepted.

"I'm a big Terry Bradshaw fan from way back," said Dallas, who later played for his father's semipro football team, the Roanoke Rush, in Virginia. "[Ben is] a big, strong guy like Terry and fit the mold of a Steelers player in my mind. He went to a small school and was a little bit of an underdog."

Against the Dolphins that rainy day, Roethlisberger moved well in the pocket to avoid Miami's fierce pass rush and steadily guided the Steelers down the field to the 7. On the next play, he fired a pass to Ward in the end zone with 6:16 remaining to cap the 61-yard drive for the game's only touchdown. Roethlisberger threw the pass away from the coverage and Ward dove to make the reception.

"Ben managed that game very well," Dallas said. "That pass to Ward, it was like two kids playing in a field somewhere. And they just drew that play up in the mud before the play. . . . He was a true leader in that game."

On the ensuing possession for the Dolphins, the Steelers hit quarterback A.J. Feeley. He fumbled, and inside linebacker James Farrior recovered to seal the win. Due in part to his team's stellar defense, Roethlisberger had outplayed the veteran Feeley. The

Steelers harassed Feeley throughout the game, and the quarterback responded by completing 13 of 27 passes for 137 yards with two interceptions and one fumble lost. He was also sacked three times. His frustration was clear when the Steelers stuffed him on a fourth-down play when Feeley needed less than a yard to move the sticks.

Roethlisberger avoided the costly mistakes that plagued the Dolphins, and despite the slippery ball and poor field conditions he completed 12 of 22 passes for 163 yards and the one touchdown to Ward. He was the first rookie quarterback to beat the Dolphins since the Patriots' Drew Bledsoe accomplished the feat a decade earlier.

After the game, Roethlisberger showcased a winning attitude: "It wasn't pretty at times, but we got the win," he said. And that's all anyone connected with the Steelers cared about after a 6–10 record the previous season. The Steelers and their fans had hoped that the club would get back on track, and Roethlisberger was just the quarterback to lead the team to victory. This game would just be the beginning.

17

THE ROAD (TRIP) TO DETROIT

AFC Wild-Card Playoff Game
Paul Brown Stadium
Cincinnati, Ohio
January 8, 2006

MILES SMITH COULD BE DESCRIBED as a self-made rabid Pittsburgh sports fan, attending and watching as many Steelers, Penguins, and Pirates games as possible. But some might say that he was simply destined to fall in love with the city's sports franchises.

Smith grew up in Chicago, and like many young boys he played peewee football. Instead of playing for the hometown Bears, however, Smith's league-champion team was called the Pittsburgh Steelers. The same was true in baseball, where his Little League team was the Pittsburgh Pirates.

So it was a natural progression for 12-year-old Miles when his family moved to Pittsburgh in 1978, at a time when the city was on the verge of an athletics explosion. The Steelers had already won two Super Bowls and were poised to capture consecutive titles again after the 1978 and '79 seasons. The powerful Pirates would also win the 1979 World Series crown, giving birth to the City of Champions. It was a great time to be a Pittsburgh sports fan, and young Miles Smith was just thrilled to be part of it.

"It was great to come to a city completely electrified by their sports teams," Smith said.

Smith was in his 20s when he moved away from Pittsburgh in 1988, but the Steelers' allure was powerful and drew him back from New York City in 2002. Instead of watching games in a crowded Steelers bar in Lower Manhattan or Hoboken, N.J., Smith and his brothers would be able to view each game in person.

Smith regularly attends Steelers home games—although he's still on a waiting list to become a full-fledged season-ticket holder—and he makes an occasional road trip. However, during the 2005 campaign, Smith and a group of about a dozen—including friends and family—became true road warriors, coming together to enjoy every moment of a playoff run that began against the archrival Bengals in Cincinnati.

"My wife and I went to the Cincy game and it was amazing," Smith recalled. "Two of our friends from Nashville, who also grew up as Steelers fans, met us there. We were sitting in the stands in a heavy Steelers section."

Even though Bengals officials urged their faithful not to sell tickets to Steelers fans, Paul Brown Stadium was filled with black and gold. Since the Cincinnati followers were incredibly obnoxious—going so far as to pelt anyone wearing Steelers colors with food, beer, and insults—the Steelers fans stayed strong by congregating together. Bengals fans constantly wailed the moronic "Who Dey?" chant, while the Steelers faithful replied, "We Dey."

The AFC North-champion Bengals had become more competitive since All-Pro quarterback Carson Palmer came into the league. But they still had rarely beaten the Steelers. The two split the regular-season matchups that season, but the Steelers were 9-3 against Cincinnati since 2000.

"We knew there would be emotions in this game," Steelers coach Bill Cowher said. "There was a lot that was being said leading up to this game, none of which I want to get into. We understood that this was a rivalry game."

Cowher was seen as someone who could not win the big game after dropping so many AFC championship games at home and losing in Super Bowl XXX. He had not yet coached the Steelers to a road victory in the playoffs. If the Steelers were going to qualify for

Steelers "road warriors" Miles Smith, Bronson Smith, and Lindsey Smith cheered the team to victory in Cincinnati.

the Super Bowl in February, they would need to win three straight road games. No sixth seed had ever won three straight road games and captured a Super Bowl title. The matchup with Cincinnati was a huge first step for Cowher and the Steelers, hoping to maintain the momentum they had built up in the regular-season homestretch by winning their final four games to clinch the AFC's second wild card.

The Bengals took a quick 10-0 advantage in the first quarter, as Shayne Graham kicked a 23-yard field goal and Rudi Johnson ran for a 20-yard score. However, the Bengals' bubble nearly burst on their second offensive play. While Palmer was throwing a 66-yard pass down the right sideline to Chris Henry, he was hit low by Steelers defensive end Kimo von Oelhoffen.

The long completion eventually led to the opening field goal, but Palmer suffered a torn anterior cruciate ligament in his left knee and had to be replaced by veteran Jon Kitna, who once torched the Steelers for more than 400 passing yards. Kitna guided the Bengals to leads of 10-0 and 17-7, but the Steelers eventually pressured him into four sacks and two interceptions as their offense came alive behind quarterback Ben Roethlisberger.

"Carson Palmer's a Pro Bowl quarterback," Cowher said. "Certainly, it's very tough when you lose a guy of that nature. You can't diminish that."

171

Steelers veteran running back Jerome Bettis was disheartened after Palmer's injury.

"It looked really bad," Bettis said. "I was just hoping that he would be OK. After that, we knew that Kitna is battle-tested. He's a veteran in this league, so we knew it was still going to be a tough test."

Steelers wideout Hines Ward was more matter-of-fact about the Bengals quarterback and his injury.

"It was different because when your leader goes down it takes a lot out of you, but it's a part of the game," Ward said. "In the playoffs, teams have to worry about injuries."

Still, Bengals fans—as well as the team—were reeling from the Palmer hit. Steelers fans sensed the momentum shifting back to their corner. Roethlisberger threw two touchdown passes in the second quarter, 19 yards to tailback Willie Parker and from five yards out to Ward. But Kitna connected with T.J. Houshmandzadeh for a seven-yard score to give Cincinnati a 17-14 halftime edge.

"[Kitna] made some big plays," Cowher said, "some big scrambles, and very good decision-making. We felt, at halftime, that we had taken their best shot. . . . It was only 17-14. That's not bad."

Cincinnati tried to stretch its lead when Graham attempted a 33-yard field goal in the third quarter. Long-snapper Brian St. Louis sailed the ball high to the holder, and the Steelers recovered at the 34. That mistake triggered a turnaround, as the Steelers took their first lead less than five minutes later. Roethlisberger threw deep to Antwaan Randle El, who beat safety Kevin Kaesviharn, but the Steelers wideout dropped the perfect pass in the end zone. Kaesviharn, however, was flagged for pass interference on the play, and that gave the Steelers a first down at the 5.

Bettis, who led the Steelers with 52 hard-fought yards on 10 carries, took it from there. He blasted through a big hole between left tackle and left guard and rumbled into the end zone to give the Steelers a 21-17 lead with 5:07 remaining in the third quarter.

"The big guy still has some pretty good feet," Cowher said of Bettis.

The Steelers were on a roll. They got the ball back a short time later and moved to midfield with a chance to put the game away.

Roethlisberger lined up in the shotgun formation on third down, with Randle El lined up to his left. Jeff Hartings' snap went directly to Randle El, who upon receiving the snap ran to his right, stopped, and threw back to Roethlisberger at the Steelers' 45 for a flea-flicker play. Roethlisberger pumped once, as Ward ran free underneath. Cedrick Wilson, however, was wide open at the 5, and hauled in the 43-yard touchdown connection to give the Steelers a 28-17 lead.

"We definitely needed a knockout punch," Wilson said. "It was a great call. Antwaan got the ball to Ben, and he got it downfield to me. It worked out just the way we drew it up."

Cowher said the Steelers had been working on that play for a couple months. "We've had it in there for a while and [offensive coordinator Ken Whisenhunt] made a great call in the perfect situation," Cowher said. "We're at the point now where there is no tomorrow. It was just a good call by Whis."

Roethlisberger still wasn't sure that if the play would work despite walking through it again the day before the game. But he sold it perfectly with a marvelous head fake that made some Bengals believe the ball was thrown over his head.

"I played opossum, and the corner started running after Antwaan, so I'm sitting there waiting for Antwaan to throw me the ball," Roethlisberger said. "He went about 10 yards farther than he was supposed to. The ball seemed like it was in the air forever. When I was catching [it], I saw out of the corner of my eye . . . a bunch of guys running down the field.

"But I knew they were in man coverage, and they were staying with somebody. When I caught the ball, I turned and saw two people open. It was my pick who to hit, Hines or Cedrick. I said that Hines had enough touchdowns this year, so I'm going to make up for the ones that I missed to Cedrick.

"I got it to him. I wasn't sure if Hines was going to box him out and catch it anyway, but he threw a good block and got Cedrick the touchdown. It wasn't a pretty [pass], so I thought it might get knocked [down] before it even got there."

In his second playoff go-round, Roethlisberger was extremely efficient, going 14-for-19 for 208 yards and three touchdowns, no interceptions, and a gaudy 148.7 passer rating. He had two miserable games the previous year in his first NFL season that ended in an AFC championship game loss to New England. Roethlisberger threw five interceptions in those two playoff games, including three in the loss to New England.

But this wasn't the same fresh-faced rookie who fell apart in the playoffs just one year earlier.

"We had to come out and weather the storm," Roethlisberger said. "They gave us a great shot in the beginning, really pounded it to us, made some big plays. We said let's keep scoring points when we can and take their best shot. I think we did that. We weathered it well."

The Steelers rallied from two 10-point deficits to beat the Bengals for the second time at Paul Brown Stadium that season. It was their first road playoff victory under Cowher, but they would need two more to get Bettis home to Detroit and Super Bowl XL. It was a daunting task, and the Indianapolis Colts were the next step for the Steelers.

"As the game looked [to be] well in the bag, we watched the previously obnoxious Cincinnati fans go quiet and then stream out of the stadium in anger and embarrassment," Smith said. "It was very gratifying after how obnoxious they had been outside the stadium before the game. All they could say was, 'Good luck with Indy. You're gonna get your [butts] kicked. . . .'

"I believe the entire team felt the destiny of getting Bettis to the [Super Bowl]. It was pure inspiration and destiny. [Pittsburgh] would have won, with or without Palmer."

That's the rub, though. Cincinnati fans, as well as the Bengals players and management, believed that the Steelers would not have had a chance if not for Palmer's injury.

"Obviously, [the injury] changed some things," Cincy coach Marvin Lewis said. "We had to come out and play the second half the way we played the first half—get the ball back, take them out of plays, make plays on third down. I feel like we as a football team need to learn from this. We came in here as a football team, and we need to leave here as a football team.

"We need to understand that it's about working through the tough times. You work through the critical points in the game, and you keep your eye on the target. (You) do your job. This is a lesson that we needed to learn. We handled the first part of the game, and then we let them right back in the football game."

Palmer said he knew immediately that his injury was serious, because he felt his whole knee pop. There wasn't a lot of physical pain, Palmer noted, but he added that it gave him a sickening feeling because he knew that his promising season had come to a premature end.

The Steelers' victory was their seventh in the past eight trips to Cincinnati, and this one was as physical as any against the Bengals.

"We knew it was going to be a four-quarter game," Bettis said. "I think the experience comes into play when you are down like we were, and you take their best punch. I think [our] experience was a factor in the second half."

Ward agreed, noting that the Steelers had been in these situations before. This was the first playoff game for Cincinnati in 15 years. The Steelers were much more battle tested. Only 10 Bengals had playoff experience, compared to 41 Steelers, and that paid off as the Steelers moved on to face the top-seeded Indianapolis Colts at the RCA Dome. Pittsburgh already had lost there earlier in the regular season, but they were a different team this time around.

"Well, we know what to expect, but it's a very different situation than earlier in the season," Steelers strong safety Troy Polamalu said. "We both have playoff experience, and they're very tough at home.

. . .

"The way that last Indy game started, with the bomb to Marvin Harrison, that was tough, but we were pretty solid the rest of the game. And we were in the game. But against a team that great, you can't give up too many big plays. I think this was a great test for us, facing Cincinnati, because they're a big-play team as well."

The Steelers were able to limit the Bengals' big-play potential, for the most part, with limited adjustments and better execution, Cowher said.

Roethlisberger's play clearly showed the most improvement.

"The Bengals came out and fired on all cylinders," Roethlisberger said. "They gave us a few 1-2 punches in the mouth, but we weathered the storm very well and were able to keep it under control. I told the guys we should batten down the hatches, weather this out and hopefully when it goes away we can step it up and play good football, and I think we did when it mattered."

But this was just the first step for Smith, the Steelers, and all the road warriors during their long journey to the Super Bowl in Detroit.

18

IN THE NICK OF TIME

AFC Divisional Playoff Game
RCA Dome
Indianapolis, Indiana
January 15, 2006

TERRY O'NEILL IS A FOURTH-GENERATION Pittsburgh Steelers fan, born, raised, and living in the same Pittsburgh-area house as those ancestors.

"It goes back to the 1800s, Civil War times, and all of us are diehard Steelers fans," O'Neill said. None of Terry's relatives can make that statement and mean it as literally as he does.

O'Neill likes to spend Sunday afternoons in the fall with a large group of friends at Cupka's restaurant and bar on Pittsburgh's South Side, just a mile from the team's practice facility. The group would need to be in full force on this particular day, because the Steelers were playing the high-powered Indianapolis Colts—the NFL's top team—with the winner earning a spot in the AFC championship game.

The Steelers came out strong with several quick scores and dominated the favored Colts 21–3 through three quarters to silence Indy's normally raucous crowd of nearly 58,000 spectators at the RCA Dome. Only diehard fans like O'Neill believed that the Steelers, the No. 6 and final AFC playoff seed, could do this to the NFL's No. 1 offense and a team that flirted with an undefeated regular season before finishing at 14-2.

Indy quarterback Peyton Manning reversed his team's fortunes in the fourth quarter by firing two touchdown passes, along with a two-point conversion, to get the Colts back in the game. Manning was aided by a referee's poor call, a Troy Polamalu interception that was incorrectly overturned. The Steelers held the ball for nearly two minutes and punted back to the Colts with 2:31 left and one final gasp.

"That was a wild game, very exciting, but nerve-wracking," O'Neill said. "There were a lot of things that happened. And when that referee didn't give Troy an interception, I felt a flutter in my chest. It was the second time it happened in the game. I just thought it was indigestion. It didn't hurt or anything, and it eventually went away."

The Steelers defense appeared to seal the win by pressuring Indy into minus-16 yards on four downs to set up its offense at the 2, as outside linebacker Joey Porter sacked Manning. Steelers announcer Tunch Ilkin was ready to turn out the lights on the Colts season. Ilkin, a former Steelers player, usually isn't so brash. But this game certainly was in the bag, wasn't it?

"After that fourth-down sack by Joey, I'm thinking that we won the game," Ilkin said. "We're on the 2-yard line, and I said: 'Call your travel agent, we're going to Denver.' I thought that was it."

During the ensuing commercial break, Ilkin said that superstitious producer Nick DelGreco chastised him for the comments. "He said I jinxed the team, because it wasn't over yet," Ilkin recalled. "I said: 'Are you kidding me? We're on the 2. Just give it to the Bus, and that's it.' I thought Jerome would finish it."

O'Neill and the crowd at Cupka's had the same thought: Bettis, O'Neill's favorite Steelers player, would take the handoff and smash his way in for the game-clinching touchdown. It would be a fitting end to a wacky game that the Steelers really dominated and should have won going away.

When Ilkin and Steelers play-by-play man Bill Hillgrove were back on the air, the usually staid Ilkin—a consummate professional during his playing days, as well as after them—was at it again. He believed the Bus ride would be short and sweet. As expected, Bettis took the handoff and cut to the right side, as the left side of the Indy defense quickly converged.

Little did anyone know that this was a life-and-death situation as far as the Steelers season and O'Neill were concerned. It was amazing to most that the Steelers got this far, and no one outside their fan base believed they could win at Indianapolis. The Colts were the NFL's premier team at 14-2 with a high-powered offense led by Manning, running back Edgerrin James, and wideouts Marvin Harrison, Reggie Wayne, and Brandon Stokley, and an improved defense. Also, they had already beaten the Steelers once this season at the RCA Dome, 26-7, in a *Monday Night Football* matchup.

"Nobody gave us a chance," Steelers play-by-play man Bill Hillgrove said. "The Colts had everything going for them, and the Steelers were lucky just to be there. That's the way a lot of people viewed that game. But I think our fans knew better, and I know the players did."

"I remember watching the NFL Network all week," fan Cheryl Jamis said. "None of those guys picked the Steelers. It just seemed like we didn't get any respect. That made me so mad. Everybody thought the Colts were the best team in the league, and nobody thought the Steelers would win."

Indy opened the season with a 13-0 record—including that relatively easy win against the Steelers—but played its best football during that stretch, while the Steelers appeared to be peaking at this time. They certainly were healthier than the last time the two teams met. The Colts were still a good team. That's certain, but they had some flaws that were revealed during a late-season loss to the San Diego Chargers.

"The Chargers showed that you could pressure Manning and even get to him, and the Colts just didn't have the correct blocking schemes to stop them," Ilkin said. "The Steelers run the same type of defense, so the Colts had to adjust to stop (outside linebackers) Joey Porter and Clark Haggans."

That was easier said than done. But Porter did his best to motivate the Colts. Cowher had warned his volatile linebacker to not provide opposing teams with bulletin-board material. In this case, Porter didn't listen too intently. He criticized the Colts for playing "soft" in their first meeting in November and challenged them to play smash-mouth football in the return matchup in the divisional playoff game. He also criticized the Colts for relying on trickery to win games rather than slugging it out, and called James' 124-yard performance in November a "cheap 100." It was the first time the Steelers allowed a runner to surpass the 100-yard plateau in 23 games.

If Porter was trying to bait the Colts into a pregame war of words, they didn't bite. In fact, Indy's players let their head coach handle it.

"I'm going to have to go back and watch the tape again after what Joey Porter said because I guess I didn't see the game the same way that he did," Colts coach Tony Dungy said. "But I don't think you can beat Pittsburgh without being a tough team."

In the end, the game had to be decided on the field. But there still were several other subplots to this playoff matchup. The Steelers complained after the November game that the home team piped artificial noise into the RCA Dome. The NFL did not investigate the situation.

Also, Colts officials asked ticket holders to avoid selling tickets to Steelers fans, regardless of the price, hoping that the blue-and-white clad crowd would make enough noise to block out any screaming black-and-gold followers. Bengals management did the same thing the previous week, but the "Steelers Nation" still traveled to Cincinnati to cheer their team and had a strong presence in Indianapolis as well.

And, then, there was Porter. He was still at it later in the week, running his mouth to the media. Porter can talk as good a game as any Steelers player, but he also backs it up. He would have a major role in the waning minutes of this playoff game. Porter and the Steelers defense harassed Manning throughout the game, and the linebacker had two of his team's five sacks to bury the Colts deep in their own territory on the 2-yard line.

The Steelers had the ball with a chance to ice the game, and it was time for them to take another ride on the Bus. Bettis was an inspirational story for this team and its fans the entire season. His certain Hall of Fame career was winding down, and the Steelers wanted to get him a Super Bowl ring.

But first, the Steelers had to get there, and Bettis could help them take a big step by slamming across the goal line with the clinching touchdown against the Colts. Everyone in the stadium knew that Bettis was getting the ball. The Colts certainly knew it. Linebacker Gary Brackett knew it, and cornerback Nick Harper did, too. Cowher and offensive coordinator Ken Whisenhunt called the play anyway. Bettis took the handoff from quarterback Ben Roethlisberger and rushed through the left side of the Colts line.

Watching the play develop at Cupka's, O'Neill's heart began to flutter again.

Brackett drilled Bettis, and the usually sure-handed Bus—who rarely fumbles and hadn't all season—was knocked off schedule. The ball flew through the air. Harper collected it and took off for the Indy end zone. He was on his way to a coast-to-coast touchdown run when Roethlisberger saved the day with an amazing shoestring tackle despite getting spun around at the 42.

It gets a little hazy for O'Neill after that. Amidst all the hoopla at Cupka's, he laid unconscious on the floor.

"I do have a history of hypertension in my family," O'Neill said. "Ben had to make the tackle. When he went down, I went down. I slid out of my chair. They said I slowly slid out of my chair and laid on the floor. My buddy, John Mureal, was there. And he thought I was just clowning around.

"I wasn't upset that the Steelers might lose. It hurt me more to see Jerome fumble. I was upset because I didn't want to see him end his career like that. A guy like that deserves better. I guess it was a little too much for me to handle. It was more than my heart could bear."

Fortunately for O'Neill, two Pittsburgh firefighters—Tommy Herbster and Dave Grady—were at the bar with him. They gave him CPR until paramedics arrived and took him to the hospital. A defibrillator was needed to get O'Neill's heart started again, and he woke up at UPMC Presbyterian Hospital in Pittsburgh later that day.

"I woke up in the hospital, and the doctor told me I was a lucky man," O'Neill said. "I said, 'That's great, but who are you?' Then, I asked him who won the game. He said I should be happy to be alive, but I pressed him."

O'Neill was given the good news. It's possible that even if his heart could have braved Bettis' fumble, that it might not have made it through the ensuing madness. Manning and the Colts quickly drove into scoring range to set up Mike Vanderjagt for a game-tying 46-yard field goal. However, Vanderjagt—the NFL's most accurate place-kicker of all time—jacked it wide right with 21 seconds remaining.

"I couldn't believe it," Ilkin said. "When he missed it, I said again: 'Call the travel agent back, we're going to Denver.' But I really had no doubt."

Neither did Mark Kaboly and several other sportswriters covering the game that day. Kaboly, a Steelers beat writer from the *Mckeesport Daily News*, had an even different view in the waning minutes. Actually, he had no view at all. Kaboly, attempting to make a veteran move, left the press box for the media room. He remembered how difficult it was after the November game to get downstairs because the elevators were held for Colts owner James Irsay and other club officials, as well as the coaches.

"The Steelers were way ahead, so I went downstairs to get a good spot," Kaboly said. "I really thought the game was basically over and watched the final minutes on a television in the media room."

When Brackett blasted Bettis to launch the football into the air, the crowd roared. Kaboly and those watching TV with him didn't know what happened, because the Steelers were just walking to the line of scrimmage. TV broadcasts run on an eight-second delay, so the game's defining final moments—Bettis' fumble, Harper's run, Roethlisberger's tackle, Manning's drive into field-goal range, and Vanderjagt's missed kick—were all delayed for Kaboly and his cohorts that afternoon.

"We could hear the crowd," Kaboly said. "It was loud, but we never knew why they were screaming until a few seconds later

Running back Jerome Bettis gave the Steelers a "Bus" ride to Super Bowl XL in his hometown of Detroit.

because of the delay. It was weird, something I really never experienced before to that degree."

Even those who viewed the game live, as well as the players who experienced it firsthand, would be hard-pressed to come up with an example of a game in their careers that had a wilder finish.

The Steelers were elated with the outcome, of course, but no one was happier than Bettis and one of his biggest fans, O'Neill.

"I'm alive, and the Steelers won the game," O'Neill said. "All in all, it was a pretty good experience, too, because I got to meet the Bus. Everybody's allowed to make one mistake in a thousand, and that's about what his record is (as far as fumbles are concerned).

"I really don't want Jerome Bettis to believe it was his fault that I had a heart attack. I didn't think there would ever be a better back for the Steelers after Franco Harris, but Jerome . . . he's just fantastic."

O'Neill also spoke with Bettis briefly through ESPN Radio on the Dan Patrick show. The two wished each other good luck for the future, and it turns out that things worked out pretty well for both. O'Neill had his life saved by two firefighters, while Roethlisberger saved Bettis' football life.

"Ben made a great play in terms of just kind of corralling the guy, because when you have your goal-line people in there (on offense) you don't have your fastest people in there," Bettis said.

Roethlisberger described what quickly raced through his mind.

"It's one of those things that once in a blue moon Jerome fumbles, and once in a blue moon I'm going to make that tackle," Roethlisberger said. "I turned to hand off to Jerome . . . and all of a sudden, I see the ball just go flying. My first reaction is to go get [the ball], but I knew I wasn't going to get there in time. So then it's, 'Let's try to slow him down, do something so our guys can come up and make a play.' At least that's what I thought would happen."

However, Roethlisberger's youth and athleticism paid off. He didn't just slow down Harper. He stopped him cold and gave the Steelers defense a chance.

"It was incredible," Bettis said of the tackle and subsequent missed field goal by Vanderjagt. "At that point, you assume we're going to overtime, so we have to get back and get ready to go into the game. I wasn't down or anything. I was just getting ready to go, assuming that he'd make that field goal. But when I saw it go wide right, it was just incredible."

But the game didn't have to get to that point. There were three calls (or non-calls, as it were) from the officials that benefitted the Colts. During one offensive series, there was clearly contact between an Indy defender and Steelers receiver, but no penalty was called. The gain would have put the Steelers in scoring range instead of forcing a punt.

On another play, several Colts came through the line because they believed a Steelers player moved. This would have resulted in a Steelers first down and kept the drive alive, instead of forcing a punt. However, even though replays showed that Steelers guard Alan Faneca moved ever so slightly and the Colts appeared to make contact, no penalty was called either way. Play was stopped, though, by the officials and a discussion ensued.

It got worse for the Steelers. During one Colts drive that eventually led to a touchdown, the Steelers had them stopped and could have sealed the win right there when Polamalu intercepted a poor Manning pass, controlled the ball, rolled over, got up, took a step, and then knocked the ball loose with his knee. Replays clearly showed in the sequence that Polamalu had control of the ball and should have retained the interception. That wasn't the ruling by the officials after watching the replay. The drive continued. The Colts eventually scored and got to within three points in the waning minutes.

All those situations led to O'Neill's heart "flutters" and forced him to eventually get a pacemaker installed, he said. "The last play there, that was the last straw. I'd had enough. I couldn't take it any more. The fumble and Ben's tackle. Those were the last things I saw."

But thanks to Roethlisberger's tackle, Vanderjagt's missed field goal, and heroics by two Pittsburgh firefighters, the Steelers continued their amazing run to the Super Bowl, and Terry O'Neill was able to watch it. Thankfully for O'Neill, his heart was up to the task.

19

NOT TO BE DENIED

AFC Championship Game
Mile High Stadium
Denver, Colorado
January 22, 2006

MAUREEN CONTE HAS BEEN a Pittsburgh Steelers fan since she was a kid, but has some difficulty remembering exactly when that love affair actually began.

"We have a pretty big yard next to my parents' home, and my older brother, Joe, and his friends used to play pickup football games all the time," Maureen said. "I was young, but I wanted to be a part of those games."

Maureen pestered Joe and his friends to teach her about football until they finally complied, and she devoured every bit of information. Maureen wanted to learn how to throw a football and catch it, and she became fairly proficient. She didn't have the strongest arm, but eventually developed good form.

"She liked the Pirates and the Steelers, but we could only take Maureen and her friends to baseball games when they were kids," Joe said. "We couldn't get tickets to the Steelers too often. But she was really into it. As far as football went, she only wanted to go to the warm-weather games.

"But I showed her how to dress for [the cold games], and then she wanted to go to all of them. . . . We went to as many as we could until we got control of two season tickets. And then, we went to all of the home games."

While Maureen rarely got to utilize her newfound football skills, she was all too happy to share her knowledge with anyone who would listen. Friends at Quigley High School, especially the males, marveled at the wealth of football information that Maureen could provide. And her specialty was the Steelers.

"I fell in love with the Steelers," Maureen said. "They were heroes to some, but they were larger-than-life to me. They were really special. Terry Bradshaw, Lynn Swann, Mean Joe Green, John Stallworth, Franco Harris, L.C. Greenwood, Mel Blount, what a team. It was a lot of fun watching them."

Maureen was just nine and 10 years old when the Steelers won their first two Super Bowl titles. By the time the team won its next two Super Bowls in 1978 and '79, she was a seasoned football fan and serious Steelers fanatic. She put her skills as a high school cheerleader to good use.

"The cheerleaders made signs for each football game at Quigley to support the team, but I wanted to make some for the Steelers," Maureen said. "I remember one for the Super Bowl against the Rams. It said, 'No Way, LA.' That's kind of clever, isn't it? Anyway, I thought so back then."

Maureen cheered the Steelers on through four Super Bowl wins in six years, but they were all watched on television. She didn't see a Steelers game in person until her teens. Maureen's uncle, Dr. Anthony Conte, purchased four season tickets after Three Rivers Stadium opened in 1970. She and Joe got to attend a few games while they were in high school, but not too many until Uncle Tony moved away in the early 1980s. That's when Maureen and Joe snatched up a pair of tickets, because Dr. Conte's sons didn't want them.

"I couldn't wait to go to more games," Maureen said. "The Steelers had some bad teams in the '80s—the Mark Malone and Bubby Brister years—but things started to get better when Bill Cowher took over as the head coach (in 1992)."

Maureen actually moved away for a while, attending Boston

Veteran Steelers fans Maureen and Joe Conte in a famous family pose.

University from 1983-87 and staying two more years for her first post-college job. She also lived in Boca Raton, Florida for three years, but moved back in '92. Joe had been attending games with various friends during that time, but Maureen couldn't pass up a chance to move back home—and go to Steelers games on a regular basis—when a job opportunity arose in January, 1992.

Maureen and Joe cheered the Steelers through numerous playoff years and five AFC championship games at home, including two against the New England Patriots at Heinz Field. However, for Maureen and Joe, none of those games compared to the AFC championship game at Denver a decade later. They didn't plan to go, but somehow, incredibly, both ended up with tickets.

Maureen was in California for the first-round wild-card playoff game at Cincinnati, but she was home with her family to watch the second-round game with the Colts at Indianapolis. She left the next day for a business trip to Seattle and was in Denver the week before the game against the Broncos.

189

"I booked that trip in December, so it was unbelievable the way it all worked out," Maureen recalled. "The client in Seattle happened to be a huge Broncos fan, and we talked about football the whole time."

After joking with him about staying in Denver for the game, Maureen's boss came through with two game tickets. When that client couldn't go, Maureen's boss gave the tickets to other clients. He eventually secured another pair for Maureen, however, and Joe gladly flew in from Texas.

"Of course, this was all short notice for me," Joe said. "I had to fly up there on Saturday, but I had to go back Sunday night."

"On the plane going out there, I was wearing a Steelers shirt and heard all kinds of [ribbing]," Joe said. "Everyone on the flight from Dallas to Denver gave me a hard time."

While Joe was able to prepare for the game, Maureen had business suits and some casual clothes in her suitcase. She needed cold-weather gear—and as much Steelers clothing as possible—so, a box was packed at home and sent to her via express mail.

"I got it just in time, so it was great," Maureen said. "Denver, the whole city, was all decked out in Broncos stuff. There was orange everywhere."

Maureen had been in Denver four days before the care package arrived, but was limited to wearing her No. 43 Troy Polamalu Steelers jersey around town. She proudly displayed her Steelers pride, but it wasn't well received.

"The Denver fans were just so cocky," Maureen said. "They thought they were going to cream us. They weren't mean or anything like that, but they were so cocky. They thought we didn't have a chance."

Prior to the game, Joe and Maureen were amazed to find thousands of Steelers fans who were tailgating. Among the many, they easily found a taker for their extra ticket, which became available when a client's wife couldn't make it to the game.

"We saw a guy in a Steelers jacket," Maureen recalled. "He was by himself and said he just flew in from Pittsburgh. He was from the North Hills and was there with his brother and some friends. But he was the only one who needed a ticket. He thought he'd have to pay a lot of money, but we couldn't do that to a Steelers fan. We sold it to him at face value, and he was so thrilled."

Once in the stadium, however, the Contes weren't among their Steelers brethren. Their tickets were in a Denver section, among a sea of orange, but the Broncos fans were curiously kind for a while. Their hospitality steadily dwindled, though, as the game began.

"These guys on my left and this guy in front of me, the first thing they wanted to know was how we got the tickets," Joe said. "They were pissed because the guy who owned the seats—these were season ticket-holder seats—he was a super fan going all the way back to when the team started. They said he knew all about the Broncos."

The super fan's fellow season ticket holders weren't angry with the Contes, Joe said, they were more displeased with him since he apparently gave up on his team before the game. These Denver fans didn't know much about the Steelers, Joe noted. They couldn't believe the Steelers even made the playoffs, much less beat the Colts to get to this point.

"Maureen and I set them straight, though," Joe said. "We told them about the injuries and midseason slump, but that the Steelers were healthy and playing really well. . . . They didn't want to hear any of it."

That much was especially true after Broncos fans endured a rough first half. The Steelers raced to a 17-3 lead, as place-kicker Jeff Reed nailed a 47-yard field goal in the first quarter to open the scoring, and quarterback Ben Roethlisberger began to heat up in the second. The defense set up the Steelers' first touchdown when, three plays after the field goal, outside linebacker Joey Porter smacked into Denver quarterback Jake Plummer to cause a fumble. Steelers nose tackle Casey Hampton recovered at the Broncos' 39.

Roethlisberger completed a 24-yard pass to tight end Heath Miller to the 14. On third down, wideout Cedrick Wilson faked inside, and cornerback Champ Bailey bit on it. Wilson cut outside, and Roethlisberger delivered a perfect pass in the back corner of the end zone for a 12-yard score to give the Steelers a 10-0 lead on the first play of the second quarter.

"I didn't know I was going to be featured," Wilson said. "They stacked the box, and the coaches left it up to the receivers to make plays down the field. Sure, I beat him with a double move on that one, but we had to work hard to get open."

With every Steelers touchdown, the Broncos faithful began to boo their team louder. The way Roethlisberger was playing, the Steelers offense was tough to stop. As the team's catalyst, Roethlisberger walked the fine line between exuding confidence and being cocky, and Ward for one believed that the quarterback's attitude was the difference in the way the Steelers were playing in the postseason.

Roethlisberger was playing in rarified air at this point. Just for making it this far, he became the first NFL quarterback to lead consecutive teams to the AFC championship game in his first two seasons. He also had a shot to become the youngest player to win the Super Bowl if the Steelers were so fortunate.

Roethlisberger won his first 13 regular-season starts to set an NFL record for rookie quarterbacks, and he was 25-4 as a starter to this point. While he had been off-target more often than not in the previous postseason, he was having an excellent playoff run this time around. And Ward benefitted as much as any Steelers wideout from the quarterback's near pinpoint accuracy during the postseason.

Jason Elam's 23-yard field goal gave the Broncos some hope, but that waned during the Steelers' ensuing 14-play, 80-yard drive that took seven minutes, 28 seconds and ended with Jerome Bettis slamming in from the 3 behind an Alan Faneca block with 1:55 left. The Steelers would have been satisfied to go into the locker room with a two-touchdown lead at halftime, but they got the ball back just eight seconds later. Steelers cornerback Ike Taylor, who dropped 10 interceptions by his count during the regular season, held on to an errant Plummer pass on the next play from scrimmage.

The Steelers began at Denver's 38, and Willie Parker ran twice for 24 yards. Bettis scored again from 12, but a Hines Ward penalty for an illegal formation brought it back to the 17. It was a crucial mistake. But Roethlisberger made up for it with another stellar play. With just seconds left before halftime, Roethlisberger scrambled

AP IMAGES

Quarterback Ben Roethlisberger was spectacular during the Steelers run through the AFC playoffs in 2005.

away from pressure to his left and threw across his body, launching a pass over two defenders into the back of the end zone where Ward caught it for a 17-yard score. It gave the Steelers a 24-3 halftime advantage and basically ended any hope that Denver had to advance to the Super Bowl.

Denver scored two second-half touchdowns, but it wasn't enough. The Broncos didn't get into the end zone until late in the third quarter on a 30-yard pass from Plummer to Ashley Lelie.

A 30-yard pass from Roethlisberger to Wilson helped set up Reed for a 42-yard field goal and a 27-10 Steelers lead early in the fourth. Denver's Charlie Adams returned the kickoff 47 yards to the Steelers' 43, but on the next play, Steelers inside linebacker Larry Foote intercepted Plummer.

The Broncos, though, still had life as Plummer hit Lelie for 38 yards. Taylor was called for a 22-yard pass-interference penalty, and Mike Anderson ran in from the 3 to cut the lead to 10 with 7:52 left.

Many Denver fans had already left by this point, and those who stayed were disappointed when Steelers defensive end Brett Keisel crashed into Plummer to force a fumble. Travis Kirschke recovered at Denver's 17, and Roethlisberger drilled the final stake into the Broncos with a four-yard scoring run.

Steelers defensive end Kimo von Oelhoffen gave credit to the offense for winning the game after its amazing first-half performance, but the defense should get kudos as well. Along with Taylor, inside linebacker Larry Foote also picked off Plummer. He was sacked three times as well, and Denver tallied just 97 total yards rushing since it was forced to pass after the Steelers saddled the Broncos with a 24-3 halftime deficit.

"Our seats were closer to the end zone, about the 20-yard line, where there was a lot of scoring," Maureen said. "And we were on the Steelers side of the field. So, it was great, until Denver fans started throwing stuff."

"I guess a couple guys were throwing peanuts, but it wasn't that bad," Joe said. "It's just that Maureen kept waving her Terrible Towel, and I don't think they appreciated that too much."

By the end of the game, the majority of Broncos fans had gone, and the Contes moved closer to the field where other Steelers fans were congregating. Some accounts had the black-and-gold faithful in attendance at upwards of 10,000, and almost all had stayed until the end.

"We wanted to see the ceremony to accept the AFC championship trophy," Maureen said. "Joe and I sat through two at Heinz Field when the Steelers lost to New England, and the Steelers fans were so gracious."

Denver, however, wasn't in the mood. A new NFL rule changed the procedure, and if the home team didn't win the ceremony could take place in the visitors' locker room. The Broncos didn't even televise the event on the Jumbotron scoreboard so the fans could enjoy it.

"I was so mad," Maureen said. "That wasn't fair. We all waited to praise the team. They earned it, and we deserved to be able to cheer for them."

Soon thereafter, Denver security forced the Steelers fans to leave, but the celebration roared on in the club's locker room. The Steelers were back in the Super Bowl, and Bettis was going home to Detroit. The Bus, in what was expected to be his final ride, reached the big game.

"This is great," Bettis said. "I'm going home. Detroit, you better be ready. The Steelers are in the Super Bowl. This is fantastic."

"I'm really proud of this team," Steelers owner Dan Rooney said. "Coach Cowher has assured me that we're going there to win this game, and I think we can do it. It's going to be a great game."

The Contes began attempting to secure tickets for the Super Bowl as well, but to this point nothing could surpass their experience in Denver.

20

OUT OF THE SHADOWS

Super Bowl XL
Ford Field
Detroit, Michigan
February 5, 2006

KIM KALOZ WASN'T AN ORDINARY big sister by any means. The 24-year-old occasionally bossed around her younger brother Vance, 19, but she never shunned him or his friends. The two shared a common bond—Steelers football—which helped to bridge the five-year gap.

"It was great having Kim as a sister, because she knew so much about football, and we both loved the Steelers," Vance said. "One time, we were in a restaurant in Pittsburgh, and these Steelers fans all complimented her for being so knowledgeable. My friends treat her the same way."

The Steelers weren't too successful in the 1980s, posting just one 10-win season in legendary coach Chuck Noll's final years. The club's record four Super Bowl wins in six seasons in the mid-to-late 1970s were beginning to fade for some. Others, like Kim and Vance, didn't even have those memories to lose. Both were born after the Steelers stunning Super Bowl run.

Despite missing out on the team's successful streak in the '70s, brother and sister had plenty of time to relive past glory days. They grew up in a household steeped in Steelers tradition. The basement in their parents' North Huntingdon, Pennsylvania, home is adorned with Steelers paraphernalia. There's even a Steelers logo emblazoned on the basement floor.

"My dad was a high school football coach, and I was always on the sideline cheering him on," Kim said. "I was the water girl, and we watched the Steelers on TV every week. It was a lot of fun.

"My friends always said I should've been the boy in the family, because I listen to all the talk shows and sports shows. I don't consider myself to be a tomboy, but I just like football. I like the entire NFL, but the Steelers are my favorite team by far."

Kim and Vance didn't get to attend any home games until after the Steelers moved to Heinz Field and the club reached the AFC championship game in quarterback Ben Roethlisberger's rookie season. But it lost to the New England Patriots for the second time in three years at Heinz Field. Kim and Vance were primed to go to the Super Bowl after the 2004 season, but the Steelers did not comply. So the pair was ecstatic when the club reached Super Bowl XL at Detroit's Ford Field.

"Those ('70s) teams were great, but these Steelers needed to win this Super Bowl for their younger fans and to step away from all those [older teams]. And we wanted to be part of it."

Kim's stepfather and mother, Dr. David and Sue Weber, purchased Super Bowl tickets through a travel agent. Kim and Vance boarded one of two chartered fan buses at 5 a.m. at Heinz Field and left for Detroit. They were fed breakfast on the bus, but it was still morning when they arrived in Detroit. It was bitterly cold and windy when the buses pulled up to the convention center near the stadium where *NFL Live* was being broadcast.

"We called our mom and told her to watch *NFL Live*, and she saw us on TV," Kim said.

Kim and Vance went inside the stadium as early as possible and took their seats high above the end zone with the Steelers logo painted in it. As kickoff neared, the stadium began to fill with fans for both teams.

"They were all right," Vance said of the many rival Seahawks fans. "My sister and I talked to them about our teams and about the game, and they were pretty nice. They did one thing that wasn't too cool, though, because they mocked our Terrible Towel with one that said: 'Pittsburgh Sucks.' I really didn't like that."

The situation improved for Kim and Vance as the game progressed. The Steelers held a 7-3 advantage against Seattle on Roethlisberger's touchdown run near halftime, and they increased that lead when tailback Willie Parker sprinted 75 yards for a score on the opening play in the second half. The Seahawks matched that touchdown in the third to get within one score, trailing 14-10, but the Steelers had the ball early in the fourth.

"Parker's run was huge, but Seattle was still in the game," KQV Radio sports director Eric Hagman said. "There was still a lot of time left, and the score was pretty close. Anything could happen from that point."

Roethlisberger took the snap from center Jeff Hartings and handed the ball to wideout Antwaan Randle El for an end around some six minutes into the fourth quarter. A reverse to Hines Ward went for an 18-yard gain earlier in the game, and this play was devised in hopes of becoming another big play. Little did anyone know.

Randle El was completing his fourth season with the Steelers, his first as a full-time starting wideout, and he had improved every season. While his receiving skills were slow to develop, though, the former college quarterback at Indiana could do so much more. He became one of the top punt returners in the NFL and also ran back kickoffs before his wideout duties increased with the Steelers.

Randle El was inexperienced as a wide receiver when the Steelers chose him in the second round in 2002. They already had No. 1 picks Plaxico Burress and Troy Edwards on the team, and they passed up former Pitt wideout Antonio Bryant. Randle El outlasted Burress and Edwards with the Steelers, and he has been more consistent than Bryant. He couldn't overtake Ward for the No. 1 wideout spot with the Steelers, however, and this would lead him to leave via free agency after the Super Bowl.

"Hines Ward was the first player that I cheered for, and I watched a feature story on him on TV," Kim said. "It really made me like him even more. And I also met him twice. He's a very nice man. So he was the first player that attracted me to the team."

But it was Bettis—not Ward—who was the feel-good story at Super Bowl XL. The Detroit native was home for his first Super Bowl appearance in what could be his final NFL game. And the Steelers did their best to help him to succeed. Bettis got the ball repeatedly when the club neared the end zone, but he couldn't score. Roethlisberger capped that drive with his touchdown, but Bettis still made an impact. He tallied 43 yards on 14 carries.

"Jerome ran hard, and he was tough to bring down," Steelers offensive guard Alan Faneca said. "He made some nice runs, but we couldn't get him in the end zone. I guess it just wasn't in the cards for him."

Bettis wasn't in on the big play. It was called "Fake-39 Toss X, Reverse Pass," and other Steelers would rise to the occasion. Randle El took a handoff from Roethlisberger, but instead of taking the ball and running around the right end for a big gain he threw it on the run. The result was a 43-yard strike downfield to Ward who pranced into the end zone for the game-clinching score.

The Steelers had scored on the same play against the Cleveland Browns earlier in the season, and Randle El just knew it would be called during the Super Bowl. Before the game, he asked Steelers offensive coordinator Ken Whisenhunt to call his number. And Randle El's eyes lit up like a lightbulb when he heard the play called by Roethlisberger in the huddle.

"When I let it go, I just said, 'Catch it,' and Hines did," Randle El recalled.

It figures that Randle El was the first receiver in Super Bowl history to throw a touchdown pass, and it's not a surprise that the big play went to Ward. He finished with five catches for 123 yards and earned the Super Bowl MVP award. Ward was going to Disney World, but Randle El got to be on Jimmy Kimmel Live an hour after the game.

And the Steelers earned a place in history. They joined the Dallas Cowboys and San Francisco 49ers as five-time Super Bowl Champs. They became the first sixth-seeded playoff team to win a Super Bowl

AP IMAGES

Super Bowl XL MVP Hines Ward has given Steelers fans plenty of reasons to smile.

ring, and they needed to win eight consecutive games to do it after going 7-5 in the first 12. That stretch included three playoff games on the road and Super Bowl XL as the capper.

Bettis finally got his Super Bowl ring, and Steelers coach Bill Cowher—in his 14th season with the team—finally shed the tag as a big-game loser. The victory took Cowher from being just another good NFL coach to a Hall of Fame candidate.

"He's a great coach, and I love him to death," Roethlisberger said. "He and the Rooneys put together a great team here, and I'm just so proud that we were able to win it for all of them. Jerome, it was important for him, but also for Coach Cowher and the Rooneys."

The Rooney family certainly deserves credit for building a championship team, but also for sticking with Cowher when he endured a 6-10 season in 2003. Their patience paid immediate dividends. That poor year allowed the Steelers to draft

Roethlisberger with the 11th overall pick in 2004 and led to an appearance in the AFC championship game. And the following year, Cowher and the Steelers returned to the Super Bowl. But this time, they won it.

"That's what he brought me here to do," Cowher said. "It really does complete a void that's been there. Mr. Rooney is what's right about the National Football League. I'm very fortunate to work for him. He makes you work as hard as you can to succeed."

Cowher said afterward that he was as proud as anyone about the Steelers' Super Bowl dynasty run in the 1970s, but now there is a new Steelers team in a new era that finally can call itself a champion. The same can be said for Bettis, who finally was able to hoist the Super Bowl trophy. His 13-year NFL journey came to an end in his hometown, and the Super Bowl win was so sweet for Bettis that he decided to retire.

"I have played this game to win the championship," Bettis said after the game. "I'm a champion, and I think The Bus' last stop is here in Detroit."

This wasn't unexpected, especially the way Bettis ended the regular season at Heinz Field about a month earlier. In 13 seasons, the final 10 with the Steelers after being drafted by the Los Angeles-St. Louis Rams, Bettis accumulated 13,662 rushing yards, the fifth best in NFL history, scored 91 touchdowns, and became the heart and soul of one of the most prosperous franchises in the NFL. But with help from players like Roethlisberger, Ward, Randle El, and a dominant offensive line, as well as defensive stars like Troy Polamalu, Ike Taylor, James Farrior, Joey Porter and Casey Hampton, Bettis completed the journey by earning a Super Bowl ring.

"It was probably going to be the last game either way," Bettis said. "It was a situation where, physically, my body is just breaking down. The last thing I wanted to do going into a game like this or going into the season was to tell my teammates that this was the last game. I never wanted to put that kind of pressure on my teammates. So, I kept it to myself."

Kim and Vance moved close to the field to get a good view of the Vince Lombardi Trophy ceremony.

"Everybody was cheering, and confetti was flying around," Kim said. "I saved some confetti. There's a lot of great memories from that moment for me. It's the most special game I was at, and it probably will be the best ever.

"It was emotional and so amazing. It took such a long time between Super Bowl games for the Steelers, so you never know when they'll get back. But we were there, and we were thrilled to be part of it."

Just ask the Rooney family about that. The club made the transition from the beloved "Chief," Art Rooney Sr., to his son Dan during the 1970s run. And he believed the Steelers would return to the Super Bowl a lot sooner than the 15 years that separated appearances. But it took even longer to finally win that one for the thumb. That's why Dan Rooney, and his son Art II, recently promoted to be the club's president, decided to keep it separate.

They wanted to pay homage to the four Super Bowl titles in the 1970s, but also acknowledge what the 2005 team accomplished. That's why the most recent Super Bowl trophy sits by itself near the others while on display in the Art Rooney Sr. library at the team's training facility offices. And it's why the Super Bowl ring commemorating the win is also different. The first four Vince Lombardi Trophies are displayed on the ring, but they're in the background. The one for Super Bowl XL stands in the forefront.

"We wanted this one to stand out," Dan Rooney said. "The old teams were great, but this is for the new team."

Rooney accepted the Super Bowl Trophy from the NFL commissioner, and he handed it to Cowher. But the coach quickly handed it back.

"I've been waiting a long time to do this," Cowher said. "This is yours."

After he let the feeling sink in a while, he still couldn't believe it.

"It's surreal right now," Cowher said. "It's a rewarding feeling to give that trophy to Mr. Rooney. . . . I really couldn't be happier for him and the city of Pittsburgh."

Dan Rooney, as always, wanted to give something back to the fans.

"It's wonderful," he said at the trophy ceremony, "but it belongs to those people right out here. We're so thrilled to bring [the championship] back to Pittsburgh."

Some fans, like Kim and Vance, didn't have to wait. They experienced it all in one wild Sunday. And even though his Super Bowl experience spanned just a day, Vance believed it would remain with him for a lifetime.

"The memories I have from being in Detroit for Super Bowl XL, from walking around that day and the Steelers winning, those are memories I'll take with me the rest of my life," Vance said. "It was the most incredible experience I've had at a football game, and I'll never forget it."

Truly, this Steelers win was one for the ages.

21

TOMLIN QUICKLY MAKES HIS MARK

February 1, 2009

Super Bowl XLIII at Raymond James Stadium

Tampa, Florida

Pittsburgh Steelers 27, Arizona Cardinals 23

THE PITTSBURGH STEELERS HAD just two head coaches during his football-watching life, so when the franchise needed a third one Michael S. Miller was concerned. During the nearly four decades that Chuck Noll (22 seasons) and Bill Cowher (15) roamed the sideline, the standard was set quite high with five Super Bowl wins in six appearances. So, when 34-year-old Mike Tomlin was hired January 22, 2007, to be the sixteenth Steelers head coach, he had clown-sized shoes to fill.

"When Tomlin was hired by the Rooney family in 2007 to be the Steelers head coach, I was a little concerned because he was such a young coach," Miller said. "The Steelers were just one year from winning the Super Bowl, and I believed they had the team in place to win another one very soon. I thought they should have brought in a more veteran guy, but I also trusted the Rooneys. And how could you not trust them? They hired Noll and Cowher, and neither had any head-coaching experience prior to getting the Steelers job. So, I put a lot of trust in the Steelers management, because the team has had just three coaches since I started following them. That type of longevity is amazing."

It didn't take Tomlin long to cement his place among the franchise's coaching royalty. Tomlin and the Steelers won the AFC North Division with a 10-6 record in the coach's rookie season, but they lost a home playoff game to the Jacksonville Jaguars in the waning minutes, 31-29, due to some questionable officiating calls. But like his predecessors, Tomlin was not deterred. He and the Steelers kicked it up a notch in 2008 with a 12-4 record and second straight AFC North title. The Steelers were primed for a lengthy playoff run, and so were the Millers. A big Steelers party was planned, just like the ones Mike and his family held every Sunday during football season while he was growing up in the suburban Pittsburgh town of Swissvale. It was great to be a Pittsburgh sports fan in the 1970s. The Steelers won four Super Bowls in six years and were named NFL Team of the Decade. The Pirates won two World Series titles as well, and the Millers were in front of their television to celebrate all of them.

"Of course, there was no NFL Network or even ESPN when I was growing up, but we got every Steelers game on television," Miller said. "We lived in Pittsburgh, so we got the Steelers games. And that was great for a young Steelers fan like me, because my family loved the Steelers. I probably started to pay attention to them, to really pay attention, after Chuck Noll was hired. And a short time after that, they got to be pretty good. A short time after that, they got really good. The 1970s were a great time to be a young Steelers fan, and their popularity just exploded in Pittsburgh. Success in the NFL was new to our city, but the Steelers were our team. We wanted to latch on to a winner, so we wanted information on the Steelers every way that we could get it.

"Back then, there was the radio, three television network stations and the newspaper. My parents, Don and Carol, were always Steelers fans for as long as I can remember, and so was I. My sisters, Jan and Kippy, were Steelers fans, too. All five of us watched the games on Sundays or Monday nights, whenever they were on. But they mostly played on Sundays at 1 o'clock. No matter where we were or what we were doing, we had to be home in time to watch the Steelers on television. And we had a nice family room where we could watch them. It had lots of sports pictures on the walls with Pittsburgh teams and Penn

Steelers radio commentator, the legendary Myron Cope, prepares for a broadcast from the booth at Heinz Field. Cope, who passed away in 2008, broadcast Steelers games for nearly forty years.

State photos making up the motif of that room. We had some Pirates baseball stuff, too, but I remember it being mostly about football.

"First things first, we had to decide what we were eating before the game, and everything was prepared in advance," Miller added. "We had several Terrible Towels, buttons and pins, Steelers cups and mugs. And if the Steelers got on a winning streak, we ate the same thing the next week, sat in the same places and probably even wore the same clothes. We were highly superstitious. We had T-shirts and sweatshirts, plenty of team gear. And we typically turned down the sound on the TV to listen to the Steelers on the radio. We wanted to hear Myron Cope. Jack Fleming called the plays, but we wanted to know what Myron had to say. And he always had something to say. You knew you were going to get the Pittsburgh feel with Myron, and that's what we wanted to hear."

With his love for the Steelers and Penn State Nittany Lions cultivated from birth—Mike and his sister, Kippy, are PSU grads, along

PHOTO BY BRANDON MILLER

Mike Miller, seated, and son Brandon display their Steelers pride at their home in Alabama.

with their parents—it's easy to see why Mike's allegiances remained strong after he graduated from college and began a professional career at Auburn University, in Auburn, Alabama, in 1985. Mike's son, Brandon, was born five years later, and allegiances to three teams were quickly developed. Like his father, Brandon was raised to cheer for the Steelers, Penn State and Auburn, which would become his alma mater in 2012.

"Who's he going to follow down here, the Atlanta Falcons? That's about all we have in our surrounding area," Mike said. "We just don't have any professional teams in this state, unless you want to count minor-league baseball. There probably are a lot of Falcons fans, since Atlanta is just 90 miles away up U.S. Interstate 85, but there probably are just as many fans of the Packers, Cowboys and Steelers, I would say. So, we've made that drive quite a few times, 90 minutes from my house to the Georgia Dome or Turner Field or even Phillips Arena, if I really wanted to see the Hawks. But I've been in Opelika, Alabama nearly 30 years, and I just haven't found any Steelers bars down here.

"So, we'll watch them when they're on TV, and we went a couple times to watch them play the Falcons in the Georgia Dome, so that was pretty cool. Those were the only times I saw the Steelers in person until 2011."

That's when Mike saw his first Steelers game in person in Pittsburgh. He and a friend, whose family has had season tickets since 1969, saw the team play the Jacksonville Jaguars October 16 at Heinz Field. The Steelers won, 17-13, and Mike Miller—dressed in his No. 16 Jim Miller jersey, vintage 1994—was thrilled.

"I think I paid, maybe, $10 for that jersey," Mike said. "Jim Miller only played for the Steelers for a couple seasons (1994-96), so when I saw that jersey in a small sporting goods store in my area I had to get it. Hardly anybody knows who it is when I wear it, since it's my last name, too. How many Steelers fans can do that? The Steelers won that game at Heinz Field, so it was a great weekend. The Steelers won, and Penn State won. I enjoyed my weekend football trip to Pennsylvania, and then I returned home with no problems. But I did return with some nice Steelers stuff to add to my collection, stuff for my office. We also have Steelers flags and tumblers to drink from during the games."

Those glasses were rarely empty during the Steelers playoff run following the 2008 season. The Steelers beat the San Diego Chargers, 35-24, in the division round and stopped AFC North rival Baltimore in the AFC championship game at Heinz Field. It was the Steelers' third win against the Ravens that season. That set up a matchup with the Arizona Cardinals in Super Bowl 43. Tomlin praised the Cardinals, who got hot with quarterback Kurt Warner leading a high-flying offense with wideouts Larry Fitzgerald, Anquan Boldin and Steve Breaston. It was the third Super Bowl (with one win) for Warner, who threw for 4,583 yards and 30 touchdowns with 14 interceptions in 2008. Fitzgerald (1,431 yards, 12 touchdowns), Boldin (1,038 yards, 11 touchdowns) and Breaston (1,006 yards, three touchdowns) each surpassed 1,000 receiving yards with 96, 89 and 77 catches, respectively.

Steelers defensive coordinator Dick LeBeau had a spectacular unit assembled to stop Warner and the Cards. Led by the NFL defensive player of the year, outside linebacker James Harrison, the Steelers topped the league in every top defensive category, including total yardage allowed, points allowed, passing yardage allowed, first downs allowed, yards per play and yards per pass. Safeties Troy Polamalu and Ryan Clark, linebackers LaMarr Woodley and James Farrior and cornerback Ike Taylor were key players, along with unsung ends Brett Keisel and Aaron Smith. Some believed it would be crucial to stop rejuvenated running back Edgerrin James, the NFL's playoff leader with 203 rushing yards. He didn't play much earlier in the season and even talked about moving to another team the next year, but the Cardinals relied on him for tough yardage in the playoffs.

"Coming off a Super Bowl a couple years earlier, it kind of was Cowher's team for Tomlin, and I think they had the potential to go to a few of them around that time," Brandon Miller said. "And the Steelers had a strong team that year. Ben [Roethlisberger] was coming into his own, and the defense was very good. They had a lot of talent on both sides of the line. The Cardinals seemed to have a better offense than defense, so I thought the Steelers could score on them."

Steelers quarterback Ben Roethlisberger, who along with Warner had a chance to be the 10th signal-caller in NFL history to win multiple Super Bowls, believed the Cardinals presented an interesting challenge defensively as well. So, the Steelers were in agreement that victory wouldn't be an easy task. Even though he scored a touchdown in his previous Super Bowl victory with Cowher after the 2005 season, his sophomore year in the NFL, Roethlisberger was just average in that Super Bowl XL win. A big performance in this big game could elevate Roethlisberger's status in the league. Steelers left offensive tackle Max Starks believed his good friend already held that lofty spot in the NFL.

"Two Super Bowls and three AFC championship games in five years, that's quite an accomplishment for any quarterback," Starks said. "That's not an every day accomplishment by any means. So, Ben is a great quarterback with a great team around him, but you also can talk about our defense. It has to be mentioned in the same breath as the Steel Curtain defenses from the 1970s. In this modern era, to do what this defense has done, it has to be mentioned among the best as well.

But the defense and Ben, all of us, we'll talk about these things after the game and especially if we win it."

The Steelers would need contributions from every player to beat the Cardinals, and no one was more aware of that than Mike Miller.

"Sure, I knew it wasn't going to be an easy game," Miller said. "The Cardinals had a lot of talent on offense, but the Steelers defense was really good that season. And with Ben and the offense, I thought we could out-score them if it came down to some sort of shootout. I was confident about that."

The Steelers drove 71 yards to the Arizona 1-yard line after taking the opening kickoff, and Roethlisberger was the catalyst with a 38-yard pass to wideout Hines Ward and 21-yard hookup with tight end Heath Miller. On third-and-goal, Roethlisberger appeared to plunge into the end zone, but a replay challenge overruled the score to set up a fourth-down play. Tomlin played it safe and had Jeff Reed kick an 18-yard field goal. Sure, he could have taken a chance, but the Steelers would quickly be in position to score more points.

After forcing a Cardinals punt, the Steelers and Roethlisberger were on a roll again. He fired for 25 yards to wideout Santonio Holmes and hit Miller for 26 into the red zone. Holmes caught another pass for seven yards to put backup running back Gary Russell in position for a one-yard burst into the end zone. The Steelers had two possessions and a 10-0 lead early in the second quarter. They became the first NFL team to score on its first two drives since the Denver Broncos in Super Bowl XXXII. The Steelers gained 135 total yards to that point, and their defense held Arizona to just one short first down in one drive.

The Cardinals finally got untracked midway through the second quarter, as quarterback Kurt Warner and wideout Anquan Boldin connected for a 45-yard reception to move the ball from near midfield to the Steelers 1. Warner stumbled on first down, but regained his balance to toss a touchdown pass to tight end Ben Patrick to make the score 10-7. After trading punts, Roethlisberger was picked off by linebacker Karlos Dansby at the Steelers 34-yard line with 2:46 remaining in the half. The ball was tipped at the line, and Dansby made had an easy interception. Just seven plays later, the Cards drove to a first-and-goal at the 1 with time running out. With 18 seconds remaining until half-time, Warner attempted to hit Boldin with a quick-hitter for the score.

However, the pass was intercepted at the goal line by Harrison, and he took off for the opposite end zone. Thanks to his own speed and athleticism, as well as some well-timed blocks by several teammates, Harrison completed the 100-yard jaunt and collapsed into the end zone for a touchdown to give the Steelers a 17-7 halftime lead. It was the longest play in the 43-year history of the Super Bowl (but Baltimore Ravens return man Jacoby Jones snapped that mark with a 108-yard kickoff return for a touchdown in Super Bowl XLVII in 2013).

"Those last couple of yards were probably tougher than anything that I've done in my life, but probably more gratifying than anything that I've done in my football career," Harrison said.

Harrison's spectacular play nearly went for naught. He faked a blitz on the goal line, but stayed in pass coverage instead to make the pick. Warner said he didn't notice Harrison around the Cards offensive line. Harrison appeared to be tackled a couple times and nearly went out of bounds as well. Replays showed that Cardinals wideout Fitzgerald actually had a shot to tackle him short of the goal line, but teammate Antrel Rolle got in his way. Fitzgerald eventually caught Harrison at the goal line, but the two rolled into the end zone. A review by officials showed that Harrison was not stopped short, and the touchdown stood as the whistle blew to end the half. It was Steelers 17, Arizona 7.

Arizona got the ball to open the second half, but Warner and the offense sputtered again. The Steelers then proceeded to go on another long scoring drive that was boosted by three personal foul penalties against the Cards. The drive was amazing—14 plays, 79 yards and 8:39—and could have sealed a win, but the Steelers couldn't get into the end zone despite a pair of first downs inside the 10. The Steelers attempted a field goal, but another Arizona penalty gave them a second chance. That failed as well, and Reed's 21-yard field goal gave the Steelers a 20-7 lead with just 2:11 remaining in the third quarter.

After several punts back and forth, Warner guided the Cards on a spectacular 87-yard scoring drive in 3:57, as he used the no-huddle attack to perfection. Cornerback Taylor had been sticking to Fitzgerald like glue all game, but he made a leaping touchdown grab from the

1 to get Arizona to within a touchdown at 20-14. And despite getting badly outplayed for much of the game, the Cardinals were within striking distance with 7:33 remaining. The two teams traded punts, but Arizona got the better of the deal, as Ben Graham hit a clutch 34-yarder that pinned the Steelers at their own 1. Two plays later, on third-and-10, Roethlisberger appeared to get his club out of danger with a 20-yard pass to Holmes. But center Justin Hartwig was called for holding in the end zone, and the penalty gave the Cardinals a safety.

The two points made it 20-16 with 2:58 remaining. Tomlin said his play-calling didn't change, despite the safety, but the Steelers had to free kick the ball to the Cardinals and go on defense once again. Arizona got the ball at its own 36 and needed just two plays to score, as Warner threw a pass to Fitzgerald on a post route. The former Pitt standout caught it without breaking stride and blew through the Steelers secondary for a 64-yard touchdown. The Cards had their first lead, 23-20, with just 2:37 remaining. But Roethlisberger and the Steelers would get one more chance to win the franchise's sixth Lombardi Trophy.

"There wasn't too much time left, and I believed Ben could do it," Miller said. "But I probably chewed all of my fingernails by then. One deflection here or there could turn into an interception, or Ben could lose the ball on one of his scrambles. Somebody else could fumble, too, and that would be the end of it. So, I was cautiously optimistic, I guess, that the Steelers could win the game."

The potential game-winning drive began rather inauspiciously, too, as Roethlisberger took the first snap at the 22-yard line. However, a 10-yard holding penalty pushed the Steelers back to their 12, and their chances for a victory were grim. But they had Roethlisberger at the helm, and he wasn't about to quit. He passed to Holmes for 14 yards and after an incompletion, he hooked up with Holmes for another first down. Wideout Nate Washington made a special guest appearance with an 11-yard reception, and Roethlisberger ran for four yards to keep the drive going forward. The Steelers had two timeouts remaining and had to burn one there, but Roethlisberger changed the field position on the next play with a 40-yard pass to Holmes that moved the ball to the Arizona 6. The next pass fell incomplete, but second down was magical. Roethlisberger lofted one into the corner of the end zone where Holmes caught it and tip-toed the sideline for the go-ahead touchdown with 35 seconds left.

"What a great catch by Holmes and a spectacular pass by Ben," Miller said. "I thought he was in, but the second time I saw it full speed I didn't know for sure. But the replays proved that Ben put it right where it needed to be. I don't think he could make that pass again, but he made it when he needed to make it. In the biggest game of his career. And when it happened, there was a lot of yelling and screaming coming from my house. The neighbors probably wondered what was going on. That was a crazy end to the game."

After another review by officials confirmed the score, Reed kicked the extra point to give the Steelers a 27-23 lead. However, they still had to kick off to the Cardinals and Warner one more time.

"Great players step up in big-time games to make plays," Holmes said, and he added that he told Roethlisberger that he "wanted to be the guy to make the plays for this team. ... I knew it was a touchdown, 100 percent. My feet never left the ground. All I did was stand up on my toes and extend my hands."

Following the ensuing kickoff, Warner completed a 20-yard pass to Fitzgerald and a 13-yarder to J.J. Arrington, which moved the ball to the Steelers 44. With 15 seconds left, Warner prepared to attempt a Hail Mary pass, but linebacker Woodley strip-sacked Warner. Defensive end Brett Keisel recovered the forced fumble for the Steelers with five seconds left. For those who believed the play had not been reviewed, NFL official Mike Pereira explained that it was and ruled as a fumble. The Steelers had the ball, and Roethlisberger took a knee to secure the Steelers' sixth Super Bowl victory. That set an NFL record for most Super Bowl wins by a team, which surpassed the Dallas Cowboys and San Francisco 49ers. Steelers chairman Dan Rooney was asked if the team's trophy room would be a little crowded with Lombardi trophies.

"We'll do whatever we need to do," Rooney said. "We'll make room."

Holmes, who caught nine passes for 131 yards and a touchdown, including four receptions for 73 yards on that final game-winning drive, was named Super Bowl MVP. He became the sixth wide receiver to win the award and also was the third Steelers receiver to be a Super Bowl MVP. Lynn Swann received the honor after Super Bowl X, while Hines Ward was the MVP in Super Bowl XL. Tomlin was selected in fan balloting as the Motorola Coach of the Year.

The Steelers didn't even qualify for the playoffs in 2009 after a 9-7 record placed them third in the AFC North, but they came back in 2010 to finish 12-4 and win their division. In the playoffs, the Steelers beat the Baltimore Ravens, 31-24, at Heinz Field and stopped the New York Jets there as well, 24-19, in the AFC championship game to qualify for an eighth Super Bowl appearance. But this one didn't end as positively for the Steelers. Without injured Pro Bowl center Maurkice Pouncey, Roethlisberger was harassed throughout the game. The Steelers still had a chance to win the game on the final drive, but running back Rashard Mendenhall fumbled away that opportunity. And the Green Bay Packers won, 31-25, as quarterback Aaron Rodgers won MVP honors.

The Steelers were 12-4 again in 2011, but dropped a stunning 29-23 decision at Denver, as Broncos quarterback Tim Tebow threw an 80-yard touchdown pass to wideout Demaryius Thomas on the first play of overtime. They looked for redemption in 2012, but stumbled to an 8-8 record. The Steelers suffered injuries to key players like Roethlisberger, Mendenhall, Harrison, Polamalu and several offensive linemen and received inconsistent play from some key players as well, which led to the .500 record and no post-season appearance.

"They lost some players, so I think they have some work to do to get back up among the best teams in the league," Brandon Miller said. "They're not bad, but they were 8-8. So, that's not good, either. With the Ravens just winning the Super Bowl and Cincinnati on the rise, it's a real tough division. So, the Steelers could get better, and they have to build their depth to stay with the top teams. I don't know how good it can be, but it can get better. That's for sure."

Have faith Steelers Nation. This franchise has been at its best when its back was against the wall. And make no mistake, the Steelers were at a low point after 2012 with numerous losses to free agency, attrition and increased age of its most veteran players. But the Steelers still have Roethlisberger at quarterback, and the team's newest family man is still in his prime. Sure, he has a lot of miles on his leg and arm and has been battered and bruised during a career that has reached double digits in years.

The Steelers offensive line has been a reason for consternation by many fans, and it has caused some problems for Roethlisberger, but that area shouldn't be an issue in the near future. What has been a position in flux in recent years should be the team's strength with young talent spread from left tackle to right. The Steelers offensive line includes center Maurkice Pouncey, guards Ramon Foster, Kelvin Beachum and David DeCastro and tackles Mike Adams and Marcus Gilbert. The depth is thin, but the talent level has a high ceiling.

That should improve the Steelers running game as well, even though former No. 1 pick Rashard Mendenhall was jettisoned, but the offense is expected to rely on Roethlisberger and the passing game as opposed to a hard-nosed, hard-hitting defense and pound-it-out, powerful running game. That might be a change from what Steelers fans are used to and even too different for some of them to wrap their heads around, but it certainly should make for some exciting football. And that's something that the Steelers Nation deserves and should embrace.

ACKNOWLEDGMENTS

I OWE THANKS TO MANY PEOPLE, including the dedicated Steelers fans who I interviewed for each chapter. They brought this book to life and provided me with hours of enjoyable conversations. I thank former Steelers media relations director Joe Gordon for his support and assistance in contacting former players Andy Russell, Mike Wagner, Rocky Bleier, Dwight White, and L.C. Greenwood, as well as former equipment manager Tony Parisi and former head groundskeeper Steve "Dirt" Dinardo.

I also must thank the late legendary Steelers broadcaster Myron Cope for his assistance, friendship, many great stories over the years—and especially for writing his book, *Double Yoi*, which helped provide a blueprint for how to write a successful Steelers book. As a first-time author, that was much appreciated.

Andy Russell also gets special thanks for writing the foreword to this book. Andy, a successful author in his own right, did not know me before this—although we'd met some 30 years ago through a neighbor who was his business associate. Though Myron and Joe Gordon had recommended me, Andy, a quality person, was quick to help.

Current Steelers broadcasters and friends Bill Hillgrove, Tunch Ilkin, and Craig Wolfley, the players, coaches, and media relations staff deserve my thanks and appreciation as well.

My good friend and fellow sportswriter, Mike Bires, who originally was slotted to write this book, deserves much credit as well. He connected me with John Humenik, Noah Amstadter, and Travis Moran from Sports Publishing. Thanks, guys, for having faith in me.

To my friends and family members who helped with this book, whether through their Steelers stories or just by listening to mine, you're the best.

To my pet Pug, Latte Mocha, for countless days spent sleeping beside me on the couch while I typed on my laptop, you were there for every word.

And to The Steelers Nation—now that the team has One for the Thumb, plus One, it's time to work on finishing the other hand.